Principles and P   ge

'009

Principles and P   ge

D0452681

Professional Workbooks

Titles in the series:

Professional Issues in Primary Practice
ISBN: 1 903300 65 7
Price: £15

Primary ICT
ISBN: 1 903300 64 9
Price: £15

Primary English
ISBN: 1 903300 61 4
Price: £15

Primary Mathematics
ISBN: 1 903300 62 2
Price: £15

Primary Science
ISBN: 1 903300 63 0
Price: £15

Principles and Practice in the Foundation Stage
ISBN: 1 903300 67 3
Price: £15

To order, please contact our distributors:

BEBC
Albion Close
Parkstone
Poole BH12 3LL
Tel: 0845 230 9000
Fax: 01202 715556
Email: learningmatters@bebc.co.uk
www.learningmatters.co.uk

Cathy Hamilton, Susan Haywood, Sammi Gibbins, Karen McInnes and Jill Williams

Professional Workbook

Principles and Practice in the Foundation Stage

www.learningmatters.co.uk

First published in 2003 by Learning Matters Ltd.

British Library Cataloguing in Publication Data
A CIP record for this book is available from the British Library.

ISBN 1 903300 67 3

Cover design by Topics – The Creative Partnership
Project management by Deer Park Productions
Typeset by Sparks Computer Solutions Ltd – www.sparks.co.uk
Printed and bound in Great Britain by Ashford Colour Press, Gosport, Hants

Learning Matters Ltd
33 Southernhay East
Exeter EX1 1NX
Tel: 01392 215560
info@learningmatters.co.uk
www.learningmatters.co.uk

Contents

Chapter 1 General introduction

Working in the Foundation Stage

There are some key principles that underpin early childhood education: it is essential that we are honest and open about these right from the beginning of this book. We believe that practitioners' personalities and values are at the heart of their teaching and therefore we must all be able to share our belief systems, continually reflect upon them and be able to justify them in the context of our practice. Those awarded Qualified Teacher Status (QTS) must also understand and uphold the professional code of the General Teaching Council (GTC) and demonstrate the eight Standards relating to professional values and practice (DfES/TTA, 2002, *Qualifying to Teach*, page 6).

We believe that all early years practitioners should take account of the following aspects of good practice.

The child:

- is a whole being and should be treated as such;
- belongs within a family and community setting;
- has parents and carers who are his/her first teachers and the partnership between parents/carers and practitioners should continue to be central to his/her development;
- develops and learns within a social context and the nature of this must be considered in all its complexity;
- can develop and learn successfully only if he or she feels secure, valued and confident;
- has a right to a developmentally appropriate curriculum.

Practitioners:

- must respect the individuality of the child;
- must take account of the fact that each child is unique and develops and learns at a different rate, and that this is an active process;
- need to recognise that reciprocal communication is a central feature of the setting. This includes the children communicating between themselves, children and adults and between the adults themselves;
- must take responsibility for establishing and nurturing genuine partnerships with parents and carers;
- need to recognise that Foundation Stage settings are multi-disciplinary in nature and require sensitive management;
- must have a strong theoretical and practical understanding of early childhood education.

We would urge you to bear these principles in mind as you embark upon this journey as an early years practitioner.

Readership

This book is intended for a range of practitioners working within the Foundation Stage. This includes trainee teachers (from any of the various routes into teaching) who intend to work in the Foundation Stage as well as undergraduates following early childhood studies degrees, early years foundation degrees, and early years modules within education degrees. It may also be of value to those teachers who are already qualified and wish to transfer to Foundation Stage settings or classrooms.

Content of this book

The Foundation Stage has been identified as a distinct phase in all children's education for those between three years old and the end of the Reception year and is now a statutory stage of the National Curriculum for England. The principles underpinning the Foundation Stage are identified within the *Curriculum Guidance for the Foundation Stage* (QCA, 2000) and it is with these in mind that the authors have selected the following themes to discuss and explore in this book.

- ⊃ Young children as learners and enquirers.
- ⊃ Making connections in children's learning.
- ⊃ Adults and children working together.
- ⊃ Organising the environment for learning.
- ⊃ Planning for learning.
- ⊃ Observing and assessing young children.

The topic of Special Educational Needs has not been discussed as a separate theme in the book, although some reference is made to the diversity of children's learning needs in the themes on 'Young children as learners and enquirers', 'Parents and children working together' and 'Observing and assessing young children'. The reasons for not including Special Educational Needs as a discrete theme are twofold.

1 To fully address the issues surrounding children with Special Educational Needs in the Foundation Stage, with the involvement of the multi-disciplinary team this implies, would demand more space than could have been given in a general book such as this.

2 The challenge of meeting the diverse needs of young children with a range of learning approaches and who may be at differing stages of development requires much skill and attention in effective early years practice generally.

It was felt by the writers that rather than focusing on Special Educational Needs as a separate theme, and run the risk of oversimplifying the issues, it was more appropriate to refer to the general issue of diversity in young children's development and learning.

We would encourage all those using this book to ensure that they support their developing understanding across all themes and issues by reading extensively. A number of sources are identified within each chapter to support this process. Your tutor, training provider or other colleagues may recommend additional literature that enhances this theoretical base. Those readers who are training to become teachers will need to refer to *Qualifying to Teach Professional Standards for Qualified Teacher Status* (DfES/TTA, 2002).

Structure of this book

Recognising the variety of experiences and understanding that readers bring to this book, as well as the range of courses in this field of study, we have tried to ensure that the book can be used flexibly by individuals, according to their needs. We recommend that you read Chapter 2 (**pages 5 to 39**), which is a general introduction to each of the themes covered. Each theme in Chapter 2 ends with a linked needs analysis, and detailed guidance on using this can be found on **pages 5 and 6**. Completing the needs analysis for each theme will help to inform your starting point for further learning. In the first instance, however, you will need to decide on the best approach to adopt depending on your particular experience and situation.

Once you have read Chapter 2 and completed the needs analysis process, you will have a better idea of your strengths and areas for further development, and how to begin to extend your learning for each theme using Chapters 3, 4 and 5. These chapters are structured around activities within Foundation Stage settings. Chapter 3, 'Making sense of the setting', is intended for those with little experience or who are working as observers and assistants in an early years setting. Chapter 4, 'Making a contribution to the setting', is aimed at those who have increasing teaching responsibility within a setting. Those of you who are taking greater responsibility for or within a setting will find the activities in Chapter 5 relevant.

Once you have completed the appropriate activities in Chapters 3, 4 and 5, you may find it useful to go back to Chapter 2 and the needs analysis tables to check that you have the appropriate evidence of your learning. If you are training to become a teacher you will need to cross-reference your evidence to the Standards you are required to demonstrate in order to be awarded QTS. To support you in this process, these are detailed in the Appendix (**page 129**) and cross-referenced to each theme covered in the book.

Whilst reading through each chapter, you will come across margin icons that represent key features of the book.

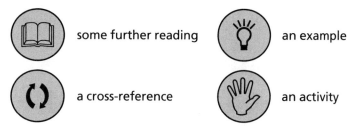

some further reading

an example

a cross-reference

an activity

Finally...

We hope you find this book a useful resource to support your understanding of Foundation Stage settings. These are complex communities and you will be reliant upon experienced practitioners as models, whilst also recognising that children will guide you in this process, if you listen to them.

It is an honour and a privilege to work with young children on a daily basis. They will challenge you, amuse you, surprise you and bring you joy, delight and infinite rewards. Enjoy their company!

Chapter 2 Guidance and needs analysis
➩ Introduction

Contents

Introduction

This chapter introduces the selected key aspects of Foundation Stage practice which are taken as themes throughout this book. The understanding of each of these themes will support you as you become a reflective early years practitioner within a Foundation Stage setting.

The contents of this section provide you with some background information for each of the themes covered. You may choose to read this section as a whole. Alternatively you may choose to select specific themes that you feel are particularly relevant or important for you to consider at this time. This will be determined by the experience you bring and the nature of the route you are following. Each theme is followed by a needs analysis table (see below for an outline of the needs analysis process). You will use the needs analysis to make a judgement about your level of professional development in relation to each theme.

The needs analysis process

Following each theme is a needs analysis to work through at your own pace, whenever you decide to audit a particular aspect of your professional understanding and practice.

Start with the column entitled 'making sense of the context' and read each of the descriptor statements listed in that column. For each one, decide if you match the descriptor and *if so* provide a date and evidence for your own records of having completed that particular element. If you do not feel confident that you can provide evidence for that descriptor then leave the evidence cell empty at this stage. Continue this process until you have considered each of the descriptor statements in the first column. If you have any evidence cells empty in the 'making sense of the context' column then it would be helpful to complete the activities contained in the matching theme at the 'making sense of the context' level in Chapter 3 (see **page 41** onwards). You will notice that some cells do not contain a descriptor. This is because the table has been constructed to demonstrate progression across the rows in the needs analysis matrix. There may not always be an appropriate description for every aspect in each theme and therefore some descriptor cells will remain empty.

Having read and completed the activities in the relevant section in Chapter 3 you will then need to return to the outstanding or empty evidence cells and complete these appropriately.

Now carry out the same process in the next column entitled 'making a contribution to the setting', and finally the same process will need to be carried out in the 'taking greater responsibility for, or within, the setting' column and descriptors.

We recommend that you photocopy these and enlarge them to A3 in order to make them easier to fill in. Below is an example of a needs analysis table with some evidence filled in. In this case, a practitioner has started to audit themselves on 'children as learners and enquirers'. You will notice that different types of evidence can be used. This could include:

➲ observations of other practitioners at work;
➲ previous experience directly related to the theme;
➲ examples of your own practice;
➲ evidence from observations by colleagues;
➲ self evaluations;
➲ reading.

Making sense of the context	Date/evidence	Making a contribution to the setting	Date/evidence	Taking a greater responsibility for or within the setting	Date/evidence
I have read the policy on teaching and learning and discussed this with my teacher	I have read the policy on teaching and learning, made notes on it and asked questions at the team meeting 12.9.03			I have discussed and updated the policy with the team as appropriate	Following observation of the children's use of the role-play area, changes were made to the policy on teaching and learning 3.4.04
I have observed the teaching of other members of the team	I have observed the teacher working with a small group 20.10.03 and the nursery nurse telling a story 22.10 03				
I have identified the theoretical basis for the teaching observed	I can recognise and analyse the principles underpinning the teaching styles and strategies that I have observed 10.02.04				
I have identified the key elements in an environment and teaching approach that enables children to feel safe and secure	From observations I have been able to recognise and analyse the aspects of the environment that contribute towards children feeling safe and secure. 3.12.03 I am beginning to understand how teaching approaches need to be adapted to ensure that all children feel safe and secure in the learning environment. 8.01.04	I understand how high emotional well-being enables children to learn effectively.	I have observed Gurprit on several occasions and she is becoming increasingly engaged in her learning now that she is settling in to the class. 21.10.03	With the team I have evaluated and reflected on how we ensure that all children feel safe and secure which enables them to take risks.	Following observations of me working with the children I have planned two new activities that seek to support children in being innovative in their play. 29.05.04 I have participated in team meetings that have reviewed how we interact with children so that they feel safe to take risks in their learning. 10.06.04

It is quite possible that through this auditing and needs analysis process you discover that you will need to work on different themes at different levels and this could be an appropriate approach for you to adopt. For example, you may need to work at the 'making a contribution to the setting' level, within the theme of 'organising the learning environment' but at a different level within the theme of 'children as learners and enquirers'. However, you may prefer to work more systematically through each level and address each theme in turn before moving on to the next level. The book is constructed to provide this kind of flexibility in its use so that it can meet the needs of different practitioners.

Chapter 2 Young children as learners and enquirers

Young children are extremely interested and curious about life and what goes on around them and have a desire to make sense of and learn about their world. Gaining an insight into how young children develop and learn, and understanding how to take children further in their learning will be a vital part of your development as an early years practitioner. This section will introduce you to the work of early years pioneers and theorists who have influenced our understanding of how young children develop and learn. It will also identify some of the elements involved in effective learning for young children. This section will cover:

- ➲ pioneers in early years education;
- ➲ child development;
- ➲ theory underpinning how young children learn;
- ➲ aspects of effective learning;
- ➲ how adults can intervene effectively in young children's learning.

The following discussion will draw upon the principles and practice outlined in the *Curriculum Guidance for the Foundation Stage* (QCA, 2000).

Pioneers in early years education

There is a strong tradition of early years education in the UK, which has influenced practice both here and across the world. Practitioners need to understand and reflect upon this tradition if they are to make sense of their work with young children. Early years practitioners are indebted to the work of Froebel (1782–1852), Montessori (1869–1952) and Steiner (1861–1925) who have all been influential on training and practice. Along with McMillan (1860–1931) and Isaacs (1885–1945) they have generated a set of core principles, which encompass the 'early childhood tradition' (Bruce, 1997; QCA, 2000).

This tradition has been built up through knowledge of how children develop and how they learn.

Child development

'Effective education requires practitioners who understand that children develop rapidly during the early years – physically, intellectually, emotionally and socially' (QCA, 2000, page11).

One of the key principles from the *Curriculum Guidance for the Foundation Stage* ensures that practitioners should have a sound knowledge of child development. Understanding how children develop can be useful to:

- ➲ identify norms of development;
- ➲ identify children's needs;
- ➲ celebrate achievements;
- ➲ identify children at risk;
- ➲ communicate with parents;
- ➲ communicate with other professionals.

Children's development can be viewed across the following six areas:

- ➲ physical development;
- ➲ intellectual development;
- ➲ language development;
- ➲ emotional development;
- ➲ social development;
- ➲ spiritual development (Bruce and Meggitt, 1999, page 25).

However, children should always be viewed holistically with all areas of development being considered as equally important.

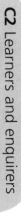
Theory underpinning how young children learn

Constructivism and social-constructivism

Constructivist theory has drawn upon the work of Jean Piaget (1896–1980). A developmental psychologist, Piaget outlined stages of development through which children progress and the process by which they learn. It is generally accepted that he underestimated the abilities of young children and his work has been critiqued by Donaldson (1978) and Tizard and Hughes (2002) who have shown children to be much more capable than Piaget thought (see Whitebread, 2003, Chapter 1 for a fuller discussion). However, early years practitioners are indebted to Piaget for showing the importance of active learning for young children and how children strive to make sense of their world.

Example: *In a small group, children actively mix water with corn flour and play with the mixture as it changes from powder to paste and then to a crumbly mix. With an adult the children discuss what they see and feel and begin to gain an understanding of changing states.*

Social constructivist theory associated with the work of Vygotsky (1986–1934) and Bruner (1915–) emphasise the social context of learning and the importance of language in learning. Vygotsky introduced the notion of 'the Zone of Proximal Development' whereby a child may reach a higher level of understanding with the help of a more knowledgeable other.

Example: *Millie is climbing up a wall with carefully prepared foot and hand holds. She is keen to get to the top, something she has never achieved before. Sophie, an older child, carefully guides her hands and feet and shouts words of encouragement to enable her to reach the top safely and proceed down the other side.*

Bruner is associated with the notion of scaffolding and the spiral curriculum. In a spiral curriculum topics or themes are revisited, over time, in order to develop a deeper level of understanding. A more knowledgeable other will scaffold the child's growing understanding through supporting and extending the child in their learning (see Whitebread, 2003, Chapter 1 for a more comprehensive discussion).

Example: *In the nursery Kirsty sings and acts out the song 'There were Ten in the Bed' with adult help. A few months later, in the Reception class Kirsty organises a group of children to sing and act out this song and helps other children to complete the process of counting back correctly.*

Multiple intelligences

Howard Gardner (1983) identified eight different types of intelligences. He claims that all human beings possess all these capacities but that each person will be more or less proficient in each one and therefore have their own unique profile. Teachers need to think about the range of learning experiences that are offered to the children in their care so as to take account of each child's differing abilities and to take them further in their learning effectively. This is discussed in more detail on **page 70.**

Example: *Children listen to the story 'We're Going on a Bear Hunt'. After hearing the story the children are invited to represent the story through drawing pictures, using musical instruments, drama or collage. Each of these media allows the children to learn in different ways: linguistically, visually, spatially and musically.*

Aspects of effective learning

Effective learning is discussed in the *Curriculum Guidance for the Foundation Stage* (QCA, 2000, pages 20 to 21). This discussion builds upon the work of the pioneers and theorists outlined above. Key aspects, which will be discussed in more detail in the subsequent chapters, are:

- ➲ active learning and first-hand experience;
- ➲ children making sense of their world;
- ➲ children feeling secure and confident as learners;
- ➲ taking risks in learning;
- ➲ different ways and rates of learning.

How adults can intervene effectively in young children's learning

Drawing upon the work and understanding of the pioneers and theorists about how young children develop and learn, teachers can then intervene more effectively in children's learning. A comprehensive breakdown of what is meant by effective teaching is given in QCA (2000, pages 22 to 24) and some of these strategies will be discussed in the following chapters, including:

- ➲ question asking;
- ➲ the development of positive attitudes to learning.

You now have a theoretical starting point for your own development and learning within this theme. You are now ready to complete the needs analysis linked to this theme in order to determine how you should proceed. You will find this overleaf on page 10.

Assessment

How far have you developed your understanding of children's development and learning? Reflect on the needs analysis table below and if possible discuss your ideas and your evidence with a colleague, teacher or tutor.

Making sense of the context	Date/evidence	Making a contribution to the setting	Date/evidence	Taking a greater responsibility for or within the setting	Date/evidence
I have read the policy on teaching and learning and discussed this with my teacher.				I have discussed and updated the policy with the team as appropriate.	
I have observed the teaching of other members of the team.					
I have identified the theoretical basis for the teaching observed.					
I have identified the key elements in an environment and teaching approach that enables children to feel safe and secure.		I understand how high emotional well-being enables children to learn effectively.		With the team I have evaluated and reflected on how we ensure that all children feel safe and secure, which enables them to take risks.	
I have identified an environment and teaching approach that enables children to engage in active learning and have first-hand experiences.				With the team I have evaluated and reflected on how we engage all children in active learning and first-hand experiences.	
		I have observed children learning and identified different rates and ways in which children learn.		I have planned, taught and reviewed with the team to ensure that activities planned for meet the learning needs of all children.	
		I have observed how members of the team interact with, and model appropriate attitudes to learning with the children.		I have interacted with the children appropriately to develop positive attitudes and dispositions to learning.	
		I have observed different types of questions being used.			
		I have observed how children respond to the questions being asked.		I can evaluate how effective my questioning is.	
If one or more of these is not yet ticked you may find it helpful to complete the activities on **pages 43 to 45**.		If one or more of these is not yet ticked you may find it helpful to complete the activities on **pages 69 to 72**.		If one or more of these is not yet ticked you may find it helpful to complete the activities on **pages 99 to 101**.	

Chapter 2 Making connections in children's learning

In the previous theme, Young children as learners and enquirers, you will have been introduced to some theoretical ideas concerning how young children learn and develop. In this theme you will take this understanding further by identifying key ways in which young children make connections in their learning and so make it meaningful. As Fisher (2002b) states, making *'connections between what is new and what has already been learnt will make secure some of the most important learning foundations for life'* (page 124).

The key ways in which children make connections in their learning are through:

➲ play;
➲ creativity;
➲ language and communication;
➲ schemas.

This section will introduce you to the above four themes and the discussion which follows will draw upon the principles and practice outlined in the *Curriculum Guidance for the Foundation Stage* (QCA, 2000).

Play

Playing is fundamental to children's development and well-being. The Early Childhood Education Forum (1998) states *'Play is essential for the healthy growth and successful development of young human beings'* (page 36). It also provides the foundation for young children's learning. QCA (2000) states that *'well-planned play, both indoors and outdoors, is a key way in which young children learn with enjoyment and challenge'* (page 25). Practitioners who work with children in the Foundation Stage would agree with this statement but all would have difficulty in defining what play is. It is possible to identify types of play and Moyles (1989, pages 12 to 13) includes a list of different types of play in school. She categorises play into three main forms: physical play, intellectual play and social/emotional play. Each form is then further subdivided. This is a useful typology of play to use when observing and understanding children at play. However, it brings us no closer to a definition of play. In fact, Moyles says that ultimately play must be seen as a process and when viewed as such a definition of play becomes impossible.

Talking about the process of play, Bruce (2001) states that *'play helps children to make connections in their learning. It helps children to bring together what they know in a connected and whole way'* (page 3). Through play children explore, practise, engage in first-hand experiences, take risks, communicate, imagine and understand the world around them. The POST Report (2000) makes clear that play enables all kinds of learning and that play should be the focus of early years education.

Creativity

Like play, creativity is a process, and has traditionally been encouraged in early years education. Also, like play, creativity is difficult to define and it is more useful to identify what creativity involves. As Duffy (1998) states, creativity is:

- *the ability to see things in fresh ways;*
- *learning from past experiences and relating this learning to new situations;*
- *thinking along unorthodox lines and breaking barriers;*
- *using non-traditional approaches to solving problems;*
- *going further than the information given;*
- *creating something unique or original* (Duffy, 1998, page 18).

Picking up on the last point Duffy (1998) alerts us to the fact that creating something new means being new to the child, not new to the world *'creativity means connecting the previously unconnected in ways that are new and meaningful to the individual concerned'* (page 18).

Example: *Deji usually works in the construction area alone building tall towers. On this occasion Sasha plays alongside him building a wall. Deji begins to construct two towers on her wall and gradually Sasha builds an enclosure around them as they work, with Deji adding towers at regular intervals. They tell the nursery nurse that they are building a castle.*

In the above example Deji actively creates something unique to him – a castle, in a way that is unique to him, by working collaboratively rather than alone.

In order to be creative children need to feel secure (Craft, 2000). Once this is achieved children engaged in the creative process will explore, take risks, communicate, be imaginative, make sense of and learn about the world around them.

Language and communication

In the previous theme you were introduced to the work of Vygotsky and Bruner. As David (1999) makes clear, both Vygotsky and Bruner view language and communication as crucial to young children's learning. At the heart of Vygotsky's notion of the 'Zone of Proximal Development' and Bruner's 'scaffolding' lies the more experienced other communicating with the child and taking the learning further. The importance of language and talking in young children's learning at home and at school has been further exemplified through the work of Wells (1986), and Tizard and Hughes (2002).

The importance of language is firmly embedded within the *Curriculum Guidance for the Foundation Stage* (QCA, 2000). This document also makes connections between language development, play and creativity in children's learning. For effective learning children need *'creative and imaginative play activities that promote the development and use of language'* (page 21).

Example: *Tony and Michael create a world for dinosaurs out of clay. They wet their hands and mould the clay to form humps and hillocks. They make a hole and add water to create a pool. They go outside and collect leaves, twigs and grass to add to their dinosaur land. As they work the teacher talks to them describing what they are doing and asking questions. They introduce dinosaurs to the land and they both become engrossed in their game using language to act out the scenario.*

Schema

Schemas are linked to the work of Piaget. A schema is defined as *'a pattern of repeatable behaviour into which experiences are assimilated and that are gradually co-ordinated. Co-ordinations lead to higher-level and more powerful schemas'* (Athey, 1990, page 37). Schemas show us how children make connections in their learning. What often appears to be random play behaviours can, through careful observation, be shown to be the exploration of connected ideas.

Example: *Megan runs around her mother in circles waiting for the nursery door to open. During the course of the morning she paints circles, which become faces and flowers. She completes a collage of circular shapes. When she goes outside she rides a trike around in circles. The nursery nurse plans an activity for Megan where she can dip balls into paint and roll them on to paper to create circular marks.*

Bruce (1997) describes different levels of schema:

➲ sensory-motor level, which is exploring schemas through the senses, actions and movements;
➲ symbolic level, which is concerned with using the schema to stand for something else;
➲ cause and effect, which is about using the schema to understand that something will happen as a result of doing something else.

Example: *In the above example with Megan she shows the sensori-motor level through walking and riding her trike around in circles. The symbolic level is shown through drawing circles to represent faces and flowers, and cause and effect is shown through ball printing.*

Assessment

You now have a theoretical starting point for your own development and learning with this theme. You are now ready to complete the needs analysis linked to this theme in order to determine how you should proceed. Reflect on the needs analysis table below and, if possible, discuss your ideas and your evidence with a colleague, teacher or tutor.

Making sense of the context	Date/evidence	Making a contribution to the setting	Date/evidence	Taking a greater responsibility for or within the setting	Date/evidence
I have a theoretical understanding of high quality play.		I can plan for learning through play.		I understand the need to value and raise the status of play.	
I am beginning to identify high quality play.		I can analyse the learning in children's play.			
I am developing a theoretical understanding of the creative process in young children's learning.		I am beginning to understand and identify cross-curricular links in children's creative behaviour.		I am gaining a deeper understanding of a creative approach to teaching and learning.	
I can identify the elements of the creative process in children's play.					
I have observed aspects of children's language development.		I can interact with, and extend, children's language in different ways.		I have observed and discussed the opportunities for children to communicate using all their expressive languages.	
I have observed adults communicating with children.					
				I can observe and identify different types of schema and I can support and extend children's schemas.	
If one or more of these is not yet ticked you may find it helpful to complete the activities on **pages 46 to 48**.		If one or more of these is not yet ticked you may find it helpful to complete the activities on **pages 73 to 76**.		If one or more of these is not yet ticked you may find it helpful to complete the activities on **pages 102 to 105**.	

Chapter 2   Adults and children working together

In this section you will learn about the ways in which adults and children can work together in nursery settings and Reception classrooms. When you first begin working in a Foundation Stage setting you will need to understand the principles which underpin the way that adults and children interact and by implication, how children are encouraged to work together.

This section will cover:

➲ practitioners and parents working together;
➲ research and practicalities relating to parental partnership;
➲ building trust and understanding including confidentiality.

The quality of relationships and communication within the setting are all-important. The Foundation Stage setting is a triangular system, where the interrelationship of the child, parent and practitioner exemplifies the ethos. Effective provision, such as the Reggio Emilia approach to early childhood education, makes this explicit in philosophy and practice.

A number of influential research projects have looked at the nature of the interaction between children, as well as that between children and adults in early years settings (Pascal and Bertram, 1997; Athey, 1990). Observing the interaction of children in one setting, Pascal and Bertram note:

> 'The resultant data indicated that fifty six per cent of interactions were between children and forty four per cent were with an adult. Eighty four per cent of the interactions were positive in tone. The children's interviews and the Involvement Observations showed that there was clearly a bonding between many of the children and the staff. Most children had a favourite member of staff. The children all knew each other well and had "best" friends too. Importantly, one member of staff noted "the staff care about each other and this provides a caring atmosphere for the children."' (Pascal and Bertram, 1997, pages 118 to 119)

Macintyre (2001) analyses child–child and child–adult relationships and expresses them respectively as vertical or horizontal. This analysis is based on the power relationships between the participants.

> 'Vertical relationships are those where the social power is unequal ... The other kind of relationships, i.e. horizontal ones are peer group friendships where cooperation and competition occur.' (Macintyre 2001, page 53)

Whilst this is true, it is vital that the ethos of the setting explicitly acknowledges the value of the child's contribution to all relationships and the benefit derived from their interaction with adults and other children. Whilst adults have authority and responsibility in the setting, children's views and perceptions must also be recognised.

Example: *A small group of children are playing with coloured water and transparent plastic tubing. The play is progressing with children talking to each other and devising their own problems to solve. The group is engrossed in the play, clearly having fun. Rather than allowing the play to continue, the trainee decides to intervene to direct the activity and take over the teaching. Later in their discussion, the class teacher suggests that the trainee may not have recognised the quality of the children's engagement in the activity, and the way that their interaction was supporting their learning.*

Learning to observe and interpret the processes of collaborative play is vital, and children's interaction with others is a significant element of this process. Children will often support and nurture each other and this competence must be recognised and valued.

When observing interactions in the setting, ask yourself whether the following statements apply:

⮑ the participants are showing respect for one another;
⮑ the tone and body language are positive;
⮑ the language used is appropriate;
⮑ differences are respected;
⮑ conflict is managed and resolved where possible.

Where adults are involved in interactions, also consider whether:

⮑ the child feels valued and his or her self-esteem is nurtured;
⮑ the child feels that he or she has been listened to.

Practitioners and parents working together

'Parents and practitioners should work together in an atmosphere of mutual respect within which children can have security and confidence.' (QCA, 2000, page 12)

This important relationship goes beyond that of simply keeping parents informed. It means involving them as fully as possible and through this process, developing a shared understanding of the child.

The importance of the relationship between parents and educators is again referred to in the *Curriculum Guidance for the Foundation Stage*:

'Parents are children's first and most enduring educators. When parents and practitioners work together in early years settings, the results have a positive impact on the child's development and learning. Therefore, each setting should seek to develop an effective partnership with parents.' (QCA, 2000, page 9)

It is also the shared view of early years practitioners as expressed by the British Association for Early Childhood Education.

'In my view, the Foundation Stage lays the foundation of the relationship between the young child, their family and the educators they meet. The Foundation Stage, at last, legitimises the importance and significance of early childhood education for the young child, its family and parents.' (Lewis, 2002, page 6)

This philosophy also underpins the provision in Scotland:

'Parents are children's prime educators in their earliest years and they continue to play a major role in their young child's learning when they enter the early years setting. Staff should value the role of parents in their children's learning and work to create a genuine partnership with them. When parents and staff work together to support children's learning, it can have significant positive effects on the way in which children value themselves and those around them.' (Scottish Consultative Council on the Curriculum, 1999, page 52)

Developing a climate of openness and exchange of information

It is widely recognised that a strong partnership between parents and educators is the most effective way to support young children's learning. (QCA, 2000, Malaguzzi, 1995; Whalley, 2001; Willey, 2001).

> 'The Froebel Early Childhood Project (Athey, 1990) was important for a number of reasons. Perhaps, most significant were involvement of parents, involvement of professional educators and the identification of effective ways of discussing children's patterns of learning with parents and sharing pedagogy.' (Nutbrown, 1999, page 135)

Nutbrown also exemplifies the value of these approaches as expressed by parents. One comments:

> 'I like going on outings with the nursery. Then when we get home we can talk about it and look at the things she collected. Then usually we bring them for you to look at with her again the next day to put on the table for the others to see too.' (Nutbrown, 1999, page 134)

Today most schools and nurseries want to work in partnership with families and welcome involvement in some form or another, and to a lesser or greater extent. This involvement may include the following examples:

⊃ open days or evenings for parents to come and play with their children, to use materials and equipment, to talk to staff and to have opportunities to understand and appreciate the importance of play to their child's overall development, and to participate in 'a two way flow of information, knowledge and expertise' (Curriculum Guidance for the Foundation Stage, page 9);
⊃ the sending of regular newsletters;
⊃ the setting up of small working parties to create and develop outdoor play spaces and work in the garden;
⊃ parties and fund-raising events;
⊃ family members helping in the classroom and with outings.

A theoretical base for parental partnership

Different settings will adopt different strategies for the partnership. Nutbrown (1999, page 140) has outlined a set of principles that should underpin the rationale for this relationship. She suggests six principles, which are:

⊃ parents are the primary carers and educators of their children;
⊃ consistency, continuity and progression;
⊃ equality of opportunity;
⊃ working in the interests of children;
⊃ respect;
⊃ the 'loving use of power' – in which she refers to Drummond's (1993) notion that rather than view power as negative, practitioners should acknowledge the power that they have in children's lives and use it positively.

It is important to take time to consider what these six principles might mean to you in terms of your own experiences and understanding at this point. Aspects of these will be explored more fully in the later chapters related to this theme.

Transition from home to setting

Children often find themselves being parted from family members for the first time when they start to attend nursery or school. For many, this transition occurs with great anticipation, excitement and no apparent upset. For some, initial bewilderment or anger at being left in a strange environment, with unfamiliar people is quickly subsumed into the realisation of the possibilities of the new situation and uncertainty is replaced with fascination and concentration. For a few, the settling in period is a long and difficult one, requiring much patience and understanding from practitioners working with them. The separation often proves even more traumatic for the parent or carer, who may need a great deal of support and reassurance.

Example: *It is the third week of the new nursery year. Most children have settled in and happily watch their parents leave. David clings to his mother. She reassures him and sits down with him on the carpet. The children around them are talking to each other. After a few minutes of greetings and exchange of news, the various members of staff each take a group for a story. It has previously been arranged with David's mother that she will leave during this period of general movement. She tells him that she is going. His hand has been held by a very sympathetic little boy, Hassan. David's mother quickly slips out even though her son has started to cry. Shamima, the bilingual assistant, who is taking the group takes hold of his other hand and tells David that the story is about a little boy called David. The group settles down in their story space. Hassan still holds his friend's hand. The story begins. The central character's name becomes 'David'. The children soon become engrossed in the action. David smiles each time he hears his name. At the end of the story time David is settled and ready to go and play. Shamima rings his mother to let her know that all is well.*

The above example demonstrates Shamima's ability to respond sensitively to the needs of David and his mother, by using some of the many skills that she has acquired during her employment in the setting, while at the same time, continuing with the planned group activity. She has empathised with child and parent, thought quickly to employ a successful strategy, and shown commitment to the partnership between staff and parent or carer.

The ethos of the setting

The *Curriculum Guidance for the Foundation Stage* requires that:

> *'… all parents are made to feel welcome, valued and necessary through a range of different opportunities for collaboration between children, parents and practitioners.'* (QCA, 2000, page 9)

This is of vital importance. Families must feel welcome and at ease. Usually, one or more visits by the child and family members will take place prior to admission. Some practitioners make home visits, while others feel that this is intrusive and may cause embarrassment. In either case, great sensitivity must be exercised when gathering information and getting to know each other. A great deal of ongoing thought and discussion will probably be taking place, at weekly staff and planning meetings, and also, incidentally, after conversations with parents and carers, about the shared responsibility for the care, nurture and education of the child between home and the setting.

Building trust and understanding

Families are entrusting their children to people they hardly know. It is the responsibility of the staff to engender an atmosphere of trust for families. This is not always easy. Time and effort are needed to develop good relationships. Respect for others, together with a non-judgemental attitude, must be paramount. Many parents look forward to the process, and relish the development of the partnership. But some parents, whose own experiences of educational establishments and other institutions have not been very happy or successful, may present as disinterested, anxious or hostile in what they perceive as a threatening environment. Although they are desperate for their child 'to do better than I did', they may find it very difficult to overcome their lack of self-confidence in the situation and need particular understanding and support to be able to participate and contribute. They may find it easier to relate to another member of the team such as a nursery nurse or bilingual assistant.

The issue of confidentiality

Staff who care for and educate young children are in receipt of information that may be of a confidential nature and, as such, must be treated with the utmost discretion.

Parents or carers may confide in a member of the team. It may be a personal matter that they need to share with someone they feel they can trust. This must be respected. It is not an opportunity for gossip or judgemental exchanges. For example, a mother may tell you, in confidence, that she is in the early stages of pregnancy, but that she does not want other people to know at present. You must respect her wishes.

However, information concerning a child's safety may be divulged. For example, a neighbour may tell you that the parents of one of the children in the class are going out during the evening, leaving the child and a younger sibling alone in the house for long periods. You would be legally required to pass this information on to the teacher in charge, who in turn would inform the person in the school or nursery designated for child protection. The information would then be handed over to the social services department of the local authority for investigation.

Sometimes children are the subject of custody disputes. You must always check with the lead practitioner if you are in any doubt about whether a child should be handed over to the person who has arrived to collect him or her.

Other opportunities for parental involvement

Depending on the area in which you are placed there may be other agencies involved to encourage parental involvement, such as Family Literacy, Sure Start and parenting classes. There is a more detailed discussion of these initiatives in Chapter 5, **page 107**.

Assessment

How far have you developed your understanding of adults and children working together? Reflect on the needs analysis table below and if possible discuss your ideas and your evidence with a colleague, teacher or tutor.

Making sense of the context	Date/evidence	Making a contribution to the setting	Date/evidence	Taking greater responsibility for or within the setting	Date/evidence
I have read the handbook for the setting.		I have read the policy or handbook that guides the partnership with parents.			
I have gathered information about the setting, its staff and routines.		I am aware of the range of strategies used to inform parents and involve them in the setting and have analysed these.		I am aware of some of the initiatives that support families in the care and education of children.	
I understand the importance of knowing about children's medical conditions, culture, language and faith backgrounds.		I am aware of the importance of settling procedures and ways in which children are supported when making the transition from home to school.			
I have gathered important basic information about the children in the setting to ensure their safety and well-being.		I understand that developing partnership with parents demands sensitivity and enables parents to make a vital contribution.		I recognise the ways in which the local environment and community can enrich the work of the setting.	
I understand the importance of children's interaction with other children and ways in which they can be supported to develop respectful relationships.		I have observed the interactions between staff and parents at the beginning and end of sessions and recognise the nature and purpose of these.		I am aware of the safety considerations regarding trips out of, or visitors to the setting. I have planned, arranged and evaluated an event.	
I have observed children's interactions, analysed these and used this to inform my practice.		I understand the importance of working in a team, and exchanging information within the team. I have analysed the systems used for this exchange.		I recognise that the success of the setting depends on the team learning and developing together and have participated in this process.	
If one or more of these is not yet ticked you may find it helpful to complete the activities on **pages 49 to 52**.		If one or more of these is not yet ticked you may find it helpful to complete the activities on **pages 77 to 81**.		If one or more of these is not yet ticked you may find it helpful to complete the activities on **pages 106 to 108**.	

Chapter 2 — Organising the environment for learning

The learning environment plays an important part in the early education of young children. The generic term *environment* refers to physical learning spaces and to the people and ideas that contribute to learning. The framework for the environment, space, child organisation, time, content, routine, rule and ritual reflects the school ethos and wider societal issues (Williams, 2003). The learning environment needs to be *'well planned and organised'* (QCA, 2000, page 12). The discussion of this theme and the tasks in the following chapters focus mainly on what makes a learning space well planned and organised.

This section will cover:

⮕ the organisation of a well-planned environment;
⮕ the roles and responsibilities of adults and children in the learning environment;
⮕ some of the influences on the learning environment.

Organising the environment

Young children are learning all the time. They arrive in early years settings (from a range of home backgrounds) with a personal view of the world, assembled as a result of different experiences. Some of these experiences have been planned but many have occurred as a normal part of growing up. The environment in any early years setting should be organised to take account of the breadth of knowledge that children bring with them to school and should support children's quest for new information and their potential as active learners.

Each setting provides unique opportunities for supporting children's learning. If you visit several different settings that provide education for four-year-old children you may be surprised at the differences in the use of the environment. The physical organisation of the space and resources must, however, be appropriate for the children to work towards the requirements for the six areas of learning set out in the early years curriculum guidance (QCA, 2000). This usually means that there will be designated areas where there is a focus on particular aspects of learning: creative areas, investigation areas and areas that support language and literacy, as examples. Moyles (1995) and Fisher (2002) both give detailed descriptions of possible layouts and resourcing of learning environments. Whatever the pattern of organisation the environment should support:

⮕ the development of trust and mutual respect between adults and children;
⮕ the development of self-esteem and positive dispositions for learning;
⮕ play and associated active, creative and independent learning opportunities;
⮕ communication through spoken language and through other creative means;
⮕ purposeful activity that helps all children to achieve their potential;
⮕ child initiated experiences, that allow risk taking and problem solving;
⮕ adult directed activities that relate to the Foundation Stage curriculum;
⮕ opportunities for observation and assessment;
⮕ the inclusion of all children;
⮕ an independent approach to learning where teaching materials are accessible, clearly labelled and well organised.

For these aims to be realised the environment needs to be planned for flexible use that satisfies the increasing demands of active young learners. Adults and children should have an interest in developing an infrastructure that works well for all of them.

Roles and responsibilities for the learning environment

Practitioners

Adults, including teachers, nursery nurses and other professionals, should establish an ethos where independence, confidence, self-discipline and positive reinforcement are established (Asprey *et al.*, 2002). The inevitable transitions and changes that children encounter between home and a setting and between settings should be as stress free as possible. Young children need to be included in an environment where they feel secure and where they can make connections with previous experiences. Everyone who works with young children makes a contribution to the environment and helps to provide *'the structure for teaching within which children explore, experiment, plan and make decisions for themselves ...'* (QCA, 2000, page 12).

Parents and carers

Parents and carers have a personal understanding of their children's development and knowledge of their lives outside the setting. Their contribution should be welcomed and they should understand something of the ethos of the setting and how this is reflected in the organisation and management of the environment and the programme provided for teaching and learning. You will need to consider whether there is a genuine partnership between parents and practitioners. This is explored in greater depth within the theme on 'Adults and children working together' (**page 15**).

Children

Children have important contributions to make to the organisation and management of the learning environment. It is their needs and their learning that have to be taken into account. As their familiarity with the setting increases they should work in partnership with adults to maintain and develop a well-structured, creative environment that works well for them. This idea is referred to in Chapter 3 on **page 53**.

Influences on the learning environment

The nature of the setting

Children within the Foundation Stage will be learning within a variety of different types of settings. Each setting will have its unique interpretation of the environment and the curriculum. The type of setting, the training of the staff, the age of the children placed in the setting are just some of the factors contributing to the environment for learning.

The Foundation Stage and national initiatives

The Foundation Stage was introduced as a distinct phase of education for children who have reached the age of three years. Initially it was not part of the National Curriculum but since changes to legislation in 2002 the Foundation Stage has become part of the National Curriculum. This means that the Early Learning Goals now have statutory status. The *Curriculum Guidance for the Foundation Stage* (QCA, 2000) provides a progression in learning for children in the Foundation Stage. The non-statutory guidance for numeracy (DfEE, 1999 and DfES, 2002) and literacy (DfEE, 1998 and DfES, 2003) also have an influence on the layout and organisation of the learning environment.

Philosophy and tradition and the effect on the learning environment

Ideas on child rearing and early education stem from philosophical frameworks and from the work of pioneers (see the theme on 'young children as learners and enquirers' **pages 7 and 57**). The ethos and organisation of some settings will reflect a combination of these ideas that will have been modified to satisfy contemporary curriculum requirements. For example, the High/Scope curriculum from the USA was developed in the 1970s (Hohman and Weikart, 1998). The longitudinal study associated with it shows social and academic benefits and versions of the curriculum with inevitable reorganisation of the learning environment were adopted in settings in this country. There was particular enthusiasm for the balance that it introduced between adult direction and child initiation. The legacy of 'plan, do and review' and the organisation of the environment to encourage independence is an important aspect of some settings.

The influence of Local Education Authority

Every LEA will have its vision for early education and in its requirements for raising standards it will have identified priorities. The LEA will monitor and assess the quality of the provision and encourage teachers to take advantage of training opportunities. The direction that an LEA and its officers take will have considerable effect on the curriculum and the organisation of the environment in the Foundation Stage settings of the local area.

The uniqueness of learning environments

The effectiveness of the learning environment relies on people, places, resources, timing, and organisation. Teaching environments in which children flourish are those where there is tentativeness and respect in adult interaction with children and where children play a part in discussing and driving relevant organisation and management of the environment.

At this stage you should understand that each environment is unique. It will be continuously evolving according to a range of influences. To be effective there are certain principles that need to be in place as well as roles and responsibilities that will ensure that children are given the best opportunities for learning.

In Chapter 3 you are encouraged to observe in and reflect upon your environment in preparation for making a contribution and eventually assuming responsibility. You now have a theoretical starting point for your own development and learning within this theme. You are ready to complete the needs analysis linked to this theme in order to determine how to progress your learning. You will find this needs analysis on page 22.

Assessment

How far have you developed your understanding of organising the learning environment? Reflect on the needs analysis table below and if possible discuss your ideas and your evidence with a colleague, teacher or tutor.

Making sense of the context	Date/evidence	Making a contribution to the setting	Date/evidence	Taking a greater responsibility for or within the setting	Date/evidence
I have observed the organisation of the environment and have evaluated how this supports play and active learning.		I am learning, with the support of the team, how to organise and manage the aspects of the physical teaching space safely and effectively.		I am confident in working with others to develop an environment for young children where provision is made for their differing needs and where planned and purposeful activity takes place inside and outside.	
I am aware of the importance of selecting and preparing resources and ensuring their appropriateness for the needs of all children. I have carried out an audit of resources and decided how to optimise their use and how to gather additional resources to support ongoing learning.				In consultation with the team I am able to provide opportunities to develop active and independent experiences where children are able to think for themselves and manage their own learning.	
I understand the need for high expectations, good relationships and the promotion of self-control and independence.				I am confident that I can work with other staff to demonstrate and promote positive values and attitudes.	
		I am able to establish an environment where diversity is valued and where children feel included, secure and valued.		I am able to improve my own teaching by evaluating it and from evidence.	
I understand the need to plan an environment that reflects the importance of language and communication.		I am able to organise the environment to include opportunities for adults and children to listen, talk, read, write and play.		I am confident that I have made progress in planning and organising for learning across the learning areas.	
I recognise that constraints are unique to each environment and I am developing creative ideas for organisation.		I understand that the environment must be changed according to the needs of the children and the demands of the curriculum.		I can discuss the effectiveness of the environment with the team and with children and plan modifications in the light of their suggestions.	
If one or more of these is not yet ticked you may find it helpful to complete the activities on **pages 53 to 56**.		If one or more of these is not yet ticked you may find it helpful to complete the activities on **pages 82 to 83**.		If one or more of these is not yet ticked you may find it helpful to complete the activities on **pages 109 to 111**.	

Chapter 2   Planning for learning

This section will help you understand the planning process in Foundation Stage settings and classrooms. As a Foundation Stage practitioner you will need to understand the different elements of planning, and how you can initiate activities and also respond to children's own ideas, experiences and, sometimes, misunderstandings to plan a balanced and challenging curriculum. The influences on planning will be discussed, including the *Curriculum Guidance for the Foundation Stage* and different philosophical approaches to the education of young children. This section will discuss:

- ⊃ the relationship between planning and learning;
- ⊃ the planning process;
- ⊃ planning for the indoor and outdoor environment;
- ⊃ planning for play;
- ⊃ informing and involving parents.

The six areas of learning

As the *Curriculum Guidance for the Foundation Stage* is structured around six areas of learning, these should be reflected in any planning for nursery and Reception classes. This contrasts with the subject basis of the curriculum for children aged six and older, and is a much more holistic approach to their education. The six areas of learning are:

- ⊃ personal, social and emotional development;
- ⊃ communication, language and literacy;
- ⊃ physical development;
- ⊃ creative development;
- ⊃ mathematical development;
- ⊃ knowledge and understanding of the world.

How children learn

The nature of children's learning is reflected in a cross curricular approach to planning in the Foundation Stage. Although the guidance is expressed as six areas of learning, many activities or experiences will address several of these at any one time. Young children do not separate their learning into areas such as 'knowledge and understanding of the world' or 'creative development', still less into subjects such as science, design and technology, art or music. Children learn by making links between all their experiences and planning should reflect this.

Example: *Rosie is playing in the role-play area of the nursery, which has been turned into a café. Two children and the nursery nurse come into the café and sit down at a table. Rosie tells them that she has tea, squash and cakes, asks what they want and 'writes' their order on a notepad. Putting the pencil behind her ear she goes to the kitchen and sets a tray with three cups, saucers and spoons, carefully matching the colours. She pours pretend tea into the cups, puts three play dough cakes on each plate and tops each with a small play dough 'sweet'. Serving the tea and cakes with a flourish she tells them to "Enjoy!". She accepts some coins, which she counts into the till, before going back to the kitchen to prepare some more play dough cakes.*

The nursery nurse is able to observe Rosie's skills in the following areas of learning. She may be able to note that Rosie can do the following.

Area of learning	Learning objectives from the Stepping Stones
Personal, social and emotional development	Display high levels of involvement in activities. Persist for extended periods of time in an activity of her choosing. Initiate interactions with other people. Seek out others to share experiences. Make connections between different aspects of her life experience. Take initiative and manage developmentally appropriate tasks. Have a positive self-image and show she is comfortable with herself.
Communication, language and literacy	Use intonation, rhythm and phrasing to make her meaning clear to others. Use language for an increasing range of purposes. Begin to use talk to pretend imaginary situations. Ascribe meanings to marks. Use writing as a means of recording and communicating.
Mathematical development	Willingly attempt to count, with some numbers in the correct order. Show confidence with numbers by initiating number activities. Count up to three or four objects by saying one number for each item. Begin to represent numbers.
Knowledge and understanding of the world	Sort objects by one function. Show interest in the lives of people familiar to her.
Physical development	Explore malleable materials. Manipulate materials to achieve a planned effect. Use simple tools to effect changes to the materials.
Creative development	Engage in imaginative and role-play based on own first-hand experience. Play alongside other children who are engaged in the same theme.

Such observations enable practitioners to build on what children already know and can do when planning for future learning (QCA, 2000). The link between observation or assessment of learning and the planning process is explored further in Chapter 4, **page 93**.

Why plan?

'Good planning is the key to making children's learning effective, exciting, varied and progressive. Good planning enables practitioners to build up knowledge about how individual children learn and make progress. It also provides opportunities for practitioners to think and talk about how to sustain a successful learning environment. This process works best when all practitioners working in the setting are involved. Practitioners who work alone will benefit from opportunities to discuss their plans with others working in similar settings.' (QCA, 2001, page 2)

A lively, well run and suitably resourced nursery setting or Reception classroom should be an exciting and stimulating place to work and play for a three, four or five-year-old. When you first visit such a setting, it is easy to be misled by the apparent ease with which routines operate. But like the iceberg, which is only partly visible above the water, the early years setting relies on much that is hidden to ensure that all runs smoothly and that the provision is well suited to the needs of the children playing and learning there. The exciting yet orderly place in which these young children are developing and learning is supported by many hidden factors, including the expertise and experience of the early years practitioners and a carefully planned curriculum. In fact, nursery and Reception classes are very complex settings. They depend on the skilful contribution of a wide range of staff within the school.

Above all, the purpose of planning is to ensure that the curriculum provision in the nursery setting or Reception classroom meets the needs of the individual child. The *Curriculum Guidance for the Foundation Stage* (QCA, 2000, page 11) expresses this in its principles. It states that planning should make *'provision for different starting points from which children develop their learning, building on what they can already do'*. It should include *'relevant and appropriate content that matches the different levels of young children's needs'* and *'planned and purposeful activity that provides opportunities for teaching and learning, both indoors and outdoors'*.

There should be opportunities for children to engage in activities planned by adults and those they plan or initiate for themselves. *'Well planned, purposeful activity and appropriate intervention by practitioners will engage children in the learning process and help them make progress in their learning.'* (QCA 2000, page 11)

If the planned activities are to meet the needs of the child, then it is vital that the starting point for planning is what the child already knows and can do. This requires the Foundation Stage practitioner to have a thorough knowledge of the child's current level of development, skill or understanding. This knowledge, obtained by observation or more formal assessment, can then inform the planning process. Teaching, assessment and learning is a cyclical process, and assessment must inform planning for teaching as well as being used to evaluate its effectiveness. Some writers have expressed concern that this may not always happen:

> *'… this knowledge may not always be used to inform or to alter planning. If teachers always begin by teaching, then there is an implicit assumption that what has been planned is appropriate and that, apart from the necessity for differentiated follow-up the needs of children will be met.'* (Fisher, 2002, page 54)

Approaches to observing and assessing children are explored in more detail in Chapter 3, **page 60**.

Who contributes to Foundation Stage planning?

You will understand from the section on adults and children working together (**page 14**) that there may be a number of different school-based staff working in the Foundation Stage setting or classroom. Planning for learning is a collaborative process, and it is likely that all of these staff will contribute to medium- and short-term planning. When you join the setting the medium-term planning may already have been completed, but you should have the opportunity to join the weekly planning meetings. This collaborative approach to planning makes use of the expertise of all staff. After the general approach to teaching activities is decided in the weekly meeting individual staff may then take responsibility for planning each activity, filling in the details, producing a written plan that all can share, and organising resources. This collaborative approach will help you develop confidence in your planning. You will be able to contribute your ideas to the planning meeting and benefit from the reflections of your more experienced colleagues to refine and develop your thinking. This shared approach to planning is vital so that all members of the staff team are fully involved and informed. This is not just a question of staff having sufficient information to be able to play their part during the day. It is also vital that all members of the class or setting team fully understand the learning objectives and focus of the planned activities and can share in the professional dialogue around them. (Deveraux and Miller, 2003)

The Foundation Stage guidance and planning

The *Curriculum Guidance for the Foundation Stage* places considerable emphasis on the importance of planning. This document sets out the knowledge, skills, understanding and attitudes that children need to learn during the Foundation Stage in order to achieve the Early Learning Goals (QCA, 2000, page 5). The curriculum guidance, therefore, forms the basis for planning for children from three years old to the end of their Reception year. Additional advice on planning in the Foundation Stage was issued by the Qualifications and Curriculum Authority shortly after the curriculum guidance itself (QCA, 2001). Practitioners will also need to be aware of and take account of the National Literacy and Numeracy Strategies. This is referred to in Chapter 5 on **page 114**.

The planning process

In general, nursery and Reception classes will have long-term plans that address the breadth and balance of the curriculum on offer. The medium-term plans, usually spanning half a term and which are based on the long-term view, ensure that there is continuity between the different areas of learning, and a progressive approach to learning activities. Short-term, weekly planning then provides more detailed information. There may be whole school policies that determine or influence the format of planning. In the Foundation Stage, planning is based around the six areas of learning, with a shared theme as a focus for most activities. The following is an example of medium-term planning for a Reception class based on the theme of

'New Life'. You will see that this plan includes references to child-initiated activities. Some child-initiated activities have been anticipated; others would develop during the planned period and the planning adjusted to take account of them. Child-initiated activities are discussed later in Chapter 4 (page 85).

Learning area	Week 1	Week 2	Week 3	Week 4	Week 5
Personal, social and emotional development	Visit to the farm. Planting fast growing seeds. Shared experience of a picnic and handling food. Treating animals with care.	Caring for animals and plants.	Caring for baby animals.	Caring for human babies. Me as a baby.	Caring for animals: chicks, ducks going back to farm. What about the eggs that did not hatch?
Planning resulting from child-initiated ideas: eliciting children's experience; looking after animals at home; me as a baby.					
Communication, language and literacy	Discussion of visit, before and after. Recording the visit with digital photos and sound recordings. Non fiction texts: baby animals.	Recording the visit with drawing and writing. Role-play area: setting up the farm shop; making labels for the shop.	Role-play area: using the farm shop. Class book: the farm, the chicks and ducks.	Recording the chicks hatching: photography, drawing, writing. Mother's Day cards.	Recording the ducks hatching: photography, drawing, writing. Weather reports.
Planning resulting from child-initiated ideas: developing farm shop based on observations of children playing in it.					
Knowledge and understanding of the world	Visit to the farm: observing animals and processes; sound recordings. Fertilised eggs from farm to classroom incubator.	Observing the eggs. Observing plants: recording growth using photos and drawings; conditions needed for growth.	Observing the eggs. Recording weather. Weather patterns in spring.	Observing chicks hatching. Data handling/ICT: recording the weather. Me as a baby/me now.	Observing the chicks hatching.
Planning resulting from child-initiated ideas: follow up on the visit, based on children's responses on the day.					
Mathematical development	Sorting and classifying animals and plants.	Data handling: favourite animals; farm shop. Recording time and temperatures linked to incubation. Counting, rotation of eggs.	Observing/measuring plant growth; farm shop. Recording time and temperatures linked to incubation. Counting, rotation of eggs.	Comparative language, estimating and measuring chicks. Measuring me. Recording time and temperatures linked to incubation. Counting, rotation of eggs.	Comparative language, estimating and measuring chicks and ducks. Recording time and temperatures linked to incubation. Counting, rotation of eggs.
Planning resulting from child-initiated ideas: developing mathematical activities based on children's play in farm shop.					
Physical development	Exploring movement: movement at the farm, animals, vehicles.	Exploring movement: jumping, hopping, leaping, darting, skipping, running, bounding etc.	Movement: run, dart jump, hop, leap, bound, skip. Making enclosure for chicks when hatched (problem).	Growing/hatching movements: animals, plants. Making container to transport the chicks (problem).	Spring dance. Making enclosure for the ducks; making container to transport the ducks (problems).
Planning resulting from child-initiated ideas: enclosure/container activities based on children's response to the problems. Building farm machinery using range of construction materials.					
Creative development	Observational drawing: spring flowers (focus on structure). Exploring sounds: the farm.	Observational drawings: duck and chicken eggs; watercolours and pastels: duck and hens eggs. Exploring sounds: the farm.	Observational drawing: catkins (smudging and blending techniques).	Water colour paintings: spring flowers. Exploring sounds: chirping, cracking, hatching.	Water colour paintings: catkins. Pastel pictures: baby chicks. Spring music/sounds (composition).
Planning resulting from child-initiated ideas: developing art activities based on materials/plants provided by the children.					

Weekly planning

Weekly planning is based on the medium-term planning and likely to include information about:

- ⊃ specific learning objectives;
- ⊃ areas of learning and cross-curricular links;
- ⊃ activities;
- ⊃ key questions;
- ⊃ resources;
- ⊃ differentiation;
- ⊃ assessment;
- ⊃ the use of ICT;
- ⊃ evaluation or review.

You will probably also be expected to create individual lesson plans for each lesson or activity you deliver. Individual lesson planning is discussed in greater detail in Chapter 4, **pages 88 to 89**.

Policy and ethos of the school or setting

If you are working in a nursery or Reception class in a school, it is likely that there will be policies that underpin the planning process throughout the whole school. There may be agreed topics or content that will be covered in different year groups so as to ensure continuity or avoid repetition. In this case you will have to take account of whole-school arrangements when planning the curriculum in the Foundation Stage. Usually, planning will be a collaborative process, where staff in the same year group work together and share planning. In schools with mixed age classes or one class in each year group, planning may be shared amongst teachers from one or more year groups.

In a nursery or Reception setting planning may be undertaken across the Foundation Stage. Increasingly, there is a move towards recognising nursery and Reception as an early years continuum, with planning undertaken across the two years, so you may find that it is the nursery and Reception team who meet together to plan an integrated approach to the curriculum. This is obviously dependent on these practitioners working closely together.

In some cases you may find yourself in a class that includes Foundation Stage children and those in Year 1, and therefore in Key Stage 1 of the National Curriculum. This is a more complex and potentially difficult situation to plan for. It is widely recognised that tension may exist between the transition from the Foundation Stage to Key Stage 1 (as well as to the National Literacy and Numeracy Strategies, for which Foundation Stage guidance has been issued). Potential tensions arise between the needs of children in the Foundation Stage and the external pressures of the standards agenda (Fisher, 2002; Moyles and Robinson, 2002). Because of the desire to raise standards in schools there can be pressure on Foundation Stage practitioners to begin formal work too early in the mistaken belief that this will raise attainment. This is a difficult issue, and the practical implications for you as a practitioner are explored further in Chapter 5, **page 113**.

Planning for the learning environment

The complexity of a Foundation Stage setting requires different sorts of planning to respond to its various features. You may be planning a specific experience for a group of children whose needs have been established by observation or assessment. Alternatively, you may be planning for an area of the setting or for the use of particular resources within it, which the children will use if they choose to. You may take children's own ideas or behaviours as the starting point of your planning.

Fisher (2002) identifies three types of activity that should be planned for.

➲ *Teacher intensive activities:* these are activities in which the teacher spends focused time with a group of children and is directly and constantly engaged with them.
➲ *Teacher initiated activities:* these are activities which are carefully planned and resourced, but which do not directly involve a teacher or other adult working with the children. These activities must be worthwhile, bring about effective learning and enable children to work or play independently.
➲ *Child initiated activities:* in these activities children are free to make their own choices about the use of materials or equipment and about the processes or outcomes of that activity.

You will return to the issues of planning for adult involvement as well as child initiated activities in Chapter 5, **pages 85 and 112**.

Planning for the indoor and outdoor environment

'Outdoor activity should be seen as an integral part of early years provision and ideally should be available to children all the time. The adults planning for the class should be thinking about the indoor and outdoor areas not as separate spaces but as linked areas where a child involved in an activity may move between them, using the equipment and resources which best meet her or his needs where and when the play requires them.' (Lasenby 1990, page 5, cited in Bilton, 2002)

In a Foundation Stage setting, the outdoor environment is as important as the classroom or indoor setting. The outdoors, whether the immediate physical surroundings or the wider school environment, is an invaluable resource for learning. Bilton (2002) stresses the need to plan for the outdoor environment with as much care as when planning classroom-based activities. When planning you must take account of the whole environment and all of the resources available to the children you teach. Look again at the areas of learning and think about the additional opportunities offered when children are able to work and play outside.

When you consider the outdoor environment do not just think about the obvious learning resources such as fixed play apparatus, plants and grounds. Think also about:

➲ The colours, smells, sounds and textures of the outdoors.
➲ The effects of the weather: allow children (suitably dressed) to experience rain, wind, warmth, cold or frost.
➲ Recording outside – drawing, photographing, taking rubbings, matching colours, using playground chalks.
➲ Allowing children to work with earth, sand, stones or plants.
➲ The opportunities provided by the outdoor environment for:
  O language;
  O mathematics – number, pattern, shape, symmetry and so on;
  O technology – combining materials, building and making;
  O science – through plants and animals;
  O physical activity in relatively unrestricted spaces;
  O working with others.
➲ What happens when you are able to take indoor activities outside:
  O painting that is not restricted to paper that can fit on a painting easel, but where the children can paint on huge sheets of paper on the wall or floor, using brushes of various sizes, hands, feet and so on;
  O an outdoor water tray or a paddling pool used for water play;
  O using bubbles, windmills, balloons, chimes, kites, fabrics and other materials that move in a breeze.

Planning for play

Play, for young children, is a natural means of expression, and any Foundation Stage classroom or setting should provide an environment that is rich in opportunities for play. Play provides the context for authentic learning and enables children to become secure, valued, confident and independent in the classroom setting.

By joining in children's play, adults can maximise its potential, providing guidance and giving status to play as a learning activity.

Example: *Kate, the nursery nurse, is the 'patient' in the role-play area, which has been turned into a hospital. The children are playing at being the doctors and nurses in the hospital. Kate guides and responds to the children, by joining in their play and maximising the potential of the activity for the development of communication.*

When planning for the Foundation Stage you should think about how the staff in the setting will be deployed to guide and support children's play. In classrooms and settings where play is valued, children will also naturally involve adults in their play. Responding appropriately will help them feel secure and help develop their independence.

Example: *Anna, the Reception teacher, is sitting with a group of children who are doing an art activity. Robbie, who is very shy and has poor language skills, has being playing with the Duplo, and has made two 'mobile phones'. He brings one over to Anna and presses the buttons on his phone. Anna copies him by pressing the buttons of her phone and they have a phone conversation in which Anna is able to model language and support Robbie's developing language skills.*

Planning for play, and valuing it, gives children ownership of the learning environment and you may find that they play with materials and equipment in a completely unexpected fashion. Provided that this is done safely, it should be encouraged. Children then have a medium to express their ideas, develop creativity, decision making and problem solving skills. The importance of providing rich resources for children's play and observing the way that children use these resources is discussed in greater detail on **pages 11, 46 and 62**.

Planning activities that are achievable but challenging

It is relatively easy to plan activities that will simply occupy children for a while. Often activities such as sand and water, construction and home corner play, as well as 'table top' games and materials are part of the ongoing provision in the setting or classroom. However, these activities too should be given consideration when planning. Smidt (2002) warns of the danger of children becoming fixed in their play, if the planning for the use of such ongoing activities does not take account of the individual needs of the children.

Involving and informing parents

One of the advantages of working in a Foundation Stage setting is that you have regular and informal contact with parents and carers. You meet them at the beginning and end of the day and important events can be discussed. Most parents and carers will be interested in what their children are learning in nursery or school. Many nursery and Reception settings display copies of planning so that parents know what their children will be covering. If they are aware of what is planned, parents may also have resources they would be willing to lend or expertise they could offer.

In some settings a more structured approach to involving parents in planning is adopted. The Pen Green Centre, a multi-disciplinary centre for the under-fives undertook a major research project which aimed to involve parents in the education of their children, and in the planning and decision making processes which determined the centre's provision. Here, parents' observations of their child at home were fed into the weekly curriculum planning meetings at the centre. Likewise, observations of the children made by the staff were communicated to parents to help inform parents as they decided what activities to plan for their children at home, what presents to buy them and so on. If you would like to read more about this influential project see Whalley (2001) *Involving Parents in the Children's Learning*.

Assessment

How far have you developed your understanding of planning for learning? Reflect on the needs analysis table below and if possible discuss your ideas and your evidence with a colleague, teacher or tutor.

Making sense of the context	Date/evidence	Making a contribution to the setting	Date/evidence	Taking greater responsibility for or within the setting	Date/evidence
I understand that planning in the Foundation Stage is based on the areas of learning. I have evaluated the planning in my setting to identify the areas of learning covered.				I have read the long-term planning and relevant curriculum policies.	
		I am able to plan lessons or activities matched to the needs of the child, based on prior observation or assessment.		I understand the importance of planning for adult intervention in children's learning.	
		I understand that there are specific approaches to differentiation and I am able to differentiate my teaching appropriately.		I am aware of the issues connected with planning in mixed age classes.	
I recognise that there are different philosophical approaches to planning in the Foundation Stage and have identified these in my setting.				I am aware of the need to plan relevant activities that recognise children's own experience, cultural, faith and linguistic backgrounds.	
I have explored the approach to planning in my setting.		I understand the ways in which staff can respond to child-initiated activities.			
I have analysed and evaluated some planned activities and identified the areas of learning covered.		I have refined and adapted my teaching, based on an evaluation of children's learning.		I have produced a medium-term plan and discussed this with the Foundation Stage team.	
				I have produced weekly plans, based on my medium-term plan.	
If one or more of these is not yet ticked you may find it helpful to complete the activities on **pages 57 to 59**.		If one or more of these is not yet ticked you may find it helpful to complete the activities on **pages 84 to 90**.		If one or more of these is not yet ticked you may find it helpful to complete the activities on **pages 112 to 115**.	

Chapter 2 — Observing and assessing young children

This section on observing children and assessing their understanding will help you to consider the role of assessment and how this can be used to identify children's developmental needs and determine teaching and learning. It is important to understand the variety of assessment strategies that can be used to gather evidence of children's learning and attainment. These have different purposes and audiences. You will need to make decisions about how you carry out assessment in the Foundation Stage and use the information gathered from this to support children's development, promote learning and inform your teaching. This section will cover:

➲ What do we mean by assessment?
➲ Why assess?
➲ Principles guiding assessment in the early years.
➲ Record keeping and reporting to parents.
➲ How do we observe and assess young children?
➲ Challenges facing practitioners in this process.
➲ Background on changes and developments of the statutory assessment requirements in the Foundation Stage.

What do we mean by assessment?

Assessment should be an integral part of the learning and teaching process.

The term 'assessment' refers to all those activities undertaken by teachers, which provide information to be used as feedback to modify the teaching and learning activities in which they are engaged (Black and Wiliam, 1998, page 2).

A major review of research on classroom assessment and its impact was carried out by Black and Wiliam (1998) and summarised within the pamphlet *Inside the Black Box*. This review confirmed that if carried out effectively then informal classroom assessment with constructive feedback to children will raise levels of attainment.

Drummond (1996) says that the responsibility to assess, to watch and to understand learning is an awesome one. She goes onto explain that it is because:

'young children's learning is so complex, rich, fascinating, varied and variable, surprising, enthusiastic and stimulating, that to see it taking place, every day of the week, before ones very eyes, is one of the great rewards of the early years educator.' (Drummond and Nutbrown, 1996, page 103)

These observations help us to understand what it is that we are witnessing and to reflect on what we can learn about the individual children with whom we work. The process of assessment is based on gathering information and evidence and the interpretation of this.

Types of assessment

There are different types of assessment, each with a very different purpose.

Formative assessment
Formative assessment is often referred to as 'assessment for learning'. This is based on a practitioner's recognition that continuous assessment of children is an invaluable source of information to inform future planning. If practitioners gather evidence of children's responses then they can shape and alter their teaching to best meet their pupils' needs. This kind of assessment for learning is appropriate in all situations and helps to identify the next steps in order to build on success or strengths as well as to

correct or support weaknesses. This kind of assessment should be ongoing in early years settings or classrooms and may contribute to the evidence used to complete the Foundation Stage Profile. These profiles are discussed later in this chapter.

Diagnostic assessment

Diagnostic assessment is a particular type of formative assessment and usually related to individual children's learning. Practitioners will use this kind of assessment to explore more fully a particular child's understanding in an attempt to find out why a child is having difficulty with a specific aspect of their learning or development. However, it can also be used to determine the full extent of a child's understanding in an area or aspect of their learning that seems to be very advanced or exceptional. It is generally a more thorough form of investigation in order to gather evidence for specific intervention to support a child's learning and development.

Example: *Rhianon is frequently observed arranging sequences of toys, objects and pictures but in unsystematic ways which suggests that she may have some problems with sequencing. However, the practitioner does not want to rush to conclusions and sets up a diagnostic assessment with some structured resources to explore her thinking and understanding more fully.*

Example: *Guy has been observed counting aloud, up to large numbers, in the home corner. The practitioner is surprised and wants to explore the full extent of his understanding of the number system so she sets up a diagnostic assessment in the home corner to allow her to explore this.*

Diagnostic assessment can involve a range of professionals such as speech therapists, physiotherapists, educational psychologists and other professionals working outside the school or setting. The nature of the multi-disciplinary team working in Foundation Stage settings is more fully explored within the theme on 'Adults and children working together' in Chapter 5 on **page 106**.

Summative assessment

This kind of assessment measures the result of learning and can be viewed as 'assessment of learning'. It occurs in classrooms at the end of a phase/period of learning (such as at the end of a topic or term) or at a particular time such as the end of Key Stages 1 or 2 in the case of National Tests (commonly referred to as SATs). From September 2002 early years practitioners are required to complete the Foundation Stage Profile for all children at the end of the Reception year. This is a summary of their progress and learning at the end of the Foundation Stage and thus a record of their achievement. In some LEAs early years practitioners are recommending that the process of gathering the evidence to complete the Foundation Stage Profiles should occur throughout the Reception year and thus contribute to the ongoing formative assessment practices already in place within these settings. Further details of this profile are described later in this chapter.

Why assess?

The Assessment Reform Group (1999) has stated that:

> '...assessment which is explicitly designed to promote learning is the single most powerful tool we have for both raising standards and empowering lifelong learners.' (page 2)

This builds on the findings of Black and Wiliam (1998) in their review of the research. They confidently conclude that the quality of children's learning can be enhanced by improving formative assessment and feedback, although they recognise the complexity of this challenge. Assessment should also take account of both *what* and *how* the child learns. In this way the practitioner can focus on the curriculum content covered by the child and their understanding of this, but also evaluate how the child is learning and whether any adaptations need to be made to the teaching strategies or methods being used. All assessments should help teachers to plan more effectively. This close link between planning and assessment is highlighted in the *Curriculum Guidance for the Foundation Stage*:

'Assessment gives insights into children's interests, achievements and possible difficulties in their learning from which next steps in learning and teaching can be planned.' (QCA, 2000, page 24)

So practitioners need to use their assessment information to modify either:

⊃ the nature of the curriculum offered;

Example: *Catherine is working in the technology area and carefully sorting and sticking a range of circular or round objects onto her paper and arranging these in circles. The nursery nurse observes her at work and suggests to the rest of the team that they collect and make available to her additional circular objects, to work with in different ways. This will support her need to investigate the circular schema (see Nutbrown, 1999, for further information on schemas and Chapter 5, 'Making connections in children's learning').*

⊃ the organisation or quality of the learning environment;

Example: *The learning support assistant in a Reception class observes a group of children playing outside on the bikes and trikes. The children appear to have adopted different roles, including that of a policeman, traffic warden and fire fighter. She decides to purchase some hats to support the children in their role-play but also provides them with some bits of hose pipe and marks out a road on the play area, to use in the role-play, if they want to.*

⊃ their own practice or the teaching approaches used;

Example: *Whilst carrying out observations on one another and the children, the nursery team discover that children are often interrupted unnecessarily by adults whilst playing and working and decide to hold a meeting to discuss this issue and how they might address it.*

⊃ or a combination of any of these.

It is our responsibility as early years practitioners to use assessment information to support, extend and enrich children's learning. We also need to continually reflect upon whether we are providing appropriate environments within which this nurturing process can take place (for an activity on this, see Chapter 5, **page 110**).

It is also important to note children's attitudes to learning as this can provide valuable information about their motivation, self-esteem or even how they view themselves 'as a learner'. Through the process of assessment we have opportunities to enhance the self-esteem and individuality of each child by recognising what is distinctive and unique about them at a particular point in their development. This detailed information can be used to support each child's growth as a learner and a person. The need to regard children holistically and for practitioners to make connections across different learning areas are both issues which are discussed more fully within other chapters.

It will be helpful now to consider the principles underpinning assessment in the early years.

Principles guiding assessment in the early years

These principles are based upon the need to develop a holistic picture of the child, recognising that children explore, play and learn within a social setting.

Hurst and Lally (1992, pages 55 to 57) provide a useful framework to consider these principles of assessment.

⊃ *It is rooted in developmentally appropriate practice.* Good assessment practices are based on the assumption that children are active learners and the evidence gathered must take account of the child's own views and perceptions. Therefore, observations must note what children actually say and do rather than what we think they do.

⊃ *It occurs in contexts with which children are familiar.* Young children need to be assessed in familiar contexts, by familiar adults and using familiar tasks or resources, otherwise the evidence gathered will not be a true reflection of what the child knows, thinks or can do.

⊃ *It is based on what children can do rather than what they cannot.* This is based on a principle advocated by Bruce (1987, 1991) as well as other early years practitioners. We need to find out what children can do rather than concern ourselves with what they cannot do and this principle must be central to any assessment process or practices.

⊃ *It acknowledges that learning is not compartmentalised under subject headings.* Young children explore and bring meaning to their environment and the world and are not concerned with subject divisions. Children should be observed whilst engaged in developmentally appropriate practice which will allow them to draw upon and demonstrate their understanding and knowledge across a range of curriculum or early learning areas. It is the responsibility of the practitioner to be able to recognise and distil the aspects of their learning and understanding and then cross-reference these to different areas of learning as identified in the *Curriculum Guidance for the Foundation Stage*, if necessary.

⊃ *It recognises that young children learn best from activities that they are motivated to choose for themselves.* This does not mean that children only learn through activities that they have selected to do themselves. Instead it means that skilful teachers can plan interesting experiences and activities for children which are just as, if not more, stimulating than those children select for themselves. Assessment needs to focus on a range of activities, both those initiated by the practitioner as well as some initiated by the child.

⊃ *It stresses that children's learning and achievements are affected by the relationships they have formed with their peers and with adults.* Children need to feel safe, secure and confident in order to learn effectively. This is achieved through an environment in which there are respectful and trusting relationships between children and adults. Children will then feel able to make decisions about their learning and will be encouraged to be independent.

⊃ *It is informed by all those who know about and are interested in the development of the child.* In order to gain a view of the child as a 'whole being' assessment information needs to be gathered from a range of people who see the child in different contexts and ways. This includes parents as well as all the practitioners working with the child.

⊃ *It is rooted in principles of equality of opportunity and the celebration of diversity.* For a curriculum to be appropriate it must take account of the previous and current experiences of the child, including features of their culture and community. Therefore, practitioners must constantly review the resources available and messages conveyed in terms of inclusive practices. The learning environment must take account of and represent linguistic, cultural, ethnic and religious diversity.

It is helpful for trainees and practitioners to continually evaluate the range of assessment practices they are using in early years settings against this framework and to consider the implications for their practice if the strategies employed do not meet these principles.

Record keeping and reporting to parents

If we believe that: '*Assessment of young children must cover all aspects of a child's development and must be concerned with attitudes, feelings, social and physical characteristics*', (Hurst and Lally, 1992, page 55), then it follows that the records of this process must also encompass all aspects of their development and learning. These records will be made up of contributions from different people such as parents and carers, practitioners, other professionals working with the child, as well as from the child themselves. Records should be gathered together in a format agreed by the early years team within the setting, to cover all the different learning areas identified within the *Curriculum Guidance for the Foundation Stage* and will usually be made up of:

➲ information collected prior to entry to the setting;
➲ ongoing written observations (informal and structured);
➲ ongoing written interpretations of these observations (usually with indications of the action to be taken);
➲ checklists or records which indicate how the child is using the learning environment or opportunities on offer (usually sampled on various occasions);
➲ dated examples of achievements and work which have been commented upon or annotated to indicate their significance;
➲ dated entries of comments or contributions by the child, the parents and a range of practitioners;
➲ regular summaries of achievement and systematic assessment against the Stepping Stones and then the Early Learning Goals, identified within the *Curriculum Guidance for the Foundation Stage*;
➲ and by the end of the reception year the completed Foundation Stage Profile.

Opportunities to have ongoing conversations with parents and carers will add to the developing picture of the child as a learner and it should be recognised that this development and learning occurs within the wider community. Hurst (1996) stresses that:

'we need to involve parents in their children's education in school because without this connection between home and school schooling can become cut off from the child's deepest and most influential experiences.' (pages 95 to 96)

So it is the responsibility of the practitioner to realise these aspirations for a genuine partnership with parents and to ensure that appropriate procedures are in place to facilitate this ongoing dialogue and to value and include their contributions to the assessment and record keeping process. It is also a statutory requirement that all parents receive a written annual report and it is anticipated that in most settings this will be based on the Foundation Stage Profile, although some settings may still retain a separate reporting form for this process.

How do we observe and assess young children?

One of the key principles identified within the *Curriculum Guidance for the Foundation Stage* is that:

'practitioners must be able to observe and respond appropriately to children, informed by a knowledge of how children develop and learn and a clear understanding of possible next steps in their development and learning.' (QCA, 2000, page 11)

Drummond (1993) summarises early years assessment practices as observing children's learning, understanding it and then putting our understanding to good use. Our aim must be then, to observe and try to understand everything that children do, in their talk, their play and in the full range of activities in which they are engaged. We need to watch children interact with one another and their environment in order to create the most comprehensive picture possible of them as individuals. However, we must also bear in mind the need to develop manageable systems for achieving this, with a strong evidence base that also captures the detail necessary for this process to be meaningful.

The Rumbold Report (1990) made the following powerful analysis of the context for assessment in the early years some twelve years ago.

'We believe there is a need for guidance for educators on the achievement of more consistent and coherent approaches to observing, assessing, recording and reporting children's progress in preschool provisions ... such guidance to inform and to improve what is offered to the under fives and the early stages of the post-five provision.' (DfES, The Rumbold Report, 1990, page 17)

It is possible to see the continuing relevance of this statement across early years provision today, particularly given the challenges of teaching and assessing young children in the Foundation Stage within so many contrasting settings.

It was on the basis of research and reports such as this that the Effective Early Learning Research Project was developed. As a part of that project Pascal and Bertram (1996) developed a very helpful framework to support observation, assessment and evaluation. This framework was drawn up to take account of two key principles or beliefs:

➲ children learn within a social context;
➲ learning only takes place when young children have positive relationships with those with whom they are interacting.

So, within any setting, the framework has three key aspects or areas of focus which take account of the principles identified above.

➲ The context – in other words the features of the physical environment and how the classroom or setting is organised and arranged to support children's learning.
➲ The process – this focuses on what is happening within the setting. There are two possible observation scales on which to record these observations. The first focuses on how involved the child is in the learning process (child involvement observation scale). The second focuses instead on the involvement of the adult and how the adult interacts with the child to support and extend their learning (adult observation scale).
➲ The outcome – this considers the outcome of the learning process from three different perspectives, that of the child, the adult and the setting. The outcomes can be judged in terms of the impact on or development of any one or more of these three aspects.

It is important to understand the detail of the EEL project and you are recommended to read further in order to do this (Pascal, C. and Bertram, A. (1996) *Effective Early Learning Research Project*. Worcester: Amber Publishing).

Challenges facing practitioners when assessing

How can we avoid making value judgements?
The way we carry out observations and interpret these when assessing is based on our own value system and we cannot deny that. However, there are ways in which practitioners can improve the reliability of that process. One crucial way is to ensure that initially you simply observe, listen and record everything that you see and hear. It is important not to attempt any interpretation at this stage or to select what to note down. We do need to be prepared to be surprised by our findings and set up systems for observing which sample children engaged in a range of activities, in different settings at different periods of the day. If this is the case we may well then observe children expressing their ideas or playing in an unexpected way. This is a potentially rich source of evidence. We also need to regularly test out our own assumptions about children and the nature of the provision we make. This can occur if all the adults in the setting are involved in observations, as comparisons and discussions can then occur based on these observations. These discussions might well reveal different expectations or observations of the same child, from different adults in the setting.

Validity issues
Another key difficulty concerns the validity of the assessments being carried out. Valid assessment methods are those that assess what they are claiming to assess. Validity of assessment can be improved by drawing on a range of information about a child's attainment and progress and using a number of different assessment techniques. However, this adds to the complexity of the task and may render the process unmanageable. For those practioners working in early years settings there

are also concerns regarding when it is appropriate to make outcome judgements of this kind about a child and when this could be seen as simply indicative of their developmental level and pathway, which may be very different to their peers.

Making time for assessment and using that time effectively
It is extremely hard to make time for observations and assessment, particularly when you are not part of an early years team, and carry sole responsibility for this. However, as already mentioned, it is important to decide when, how and who you will observe when doing your planning. This should facilitate the process and ensure that it is taken into account, alongside all the other activities with which you will be engaged.

The following list of questions for practitioners was recommended by Edgington, (1998, page 168) to review these kinds of issues:

➲ How can you make relatively uninterrupted time for observations?
➲ Which methods of recording will you use?
➲ How will you share and make use of the observations made by all team members?

These issues are also explored further in Chapters 4 and 5 on **pages 91 to 95 and 116 to 120**.

'Value added' issues to demonstrate progress

There are concerns regarding how to demonstrate genuine progress of children's attainment from the Foundation Stage to Key Stage 1, and the idea of showing this development is referred to as 'value added'. The only way to provide evidence of the value added dimension is to test or assess children on entry to the school or Key Stage and then again on exit. Perhaps this is the reason why 'baseline assessment' – which used to be completed on entry to school – as well as Key Stage 1 SATs results, become essential as a basis for later comparisons of progress. It now appears that the Foundation Stage Profile evidence will also be used in this way to demonstrate the effectiveness of the teaching in a school, as measured by the children's progress between the end of the Foundation Stage and Key Stage 1 SATs Tests.

Statutory assessment

It is important to gain some understanding of the background context and development of statutory assessment requirements for Foundation Stage children over the last few years, in order to make sense of the current context.

Until September 2002 baseline assessment was compulsory for Reception children and completed in the autumn term in which they started school. The results of these baseline assessments were meant to be used 'formatively' to inform future work with individual children. However, Lindsay (1998) suggested that the purposes of baseline assessment fell into two distinct categories. The first focused on the child, in other words, asking how this child's learning and developmental needs can best be met. The second category focused on the school and the baseline assessment data was frequently used to predict a child's progress in the Key Stage 1 SATs two and a half years later. Comparisons were made with national data and projected achievement in SATs based on this information.

Since September 2002 Foundation Stage Profiles (QCA, 2003) have been introduced, which must be completed during the year and finalised in the summer term of the final year of the Foundation Stage. However, most practitioners will be collecting this evidence and information throughout the Reception year. All Foundation Stage practitioners are required to gather assessment information against the six areas of learning identified within the *Curriculum Guidance for the Foundation Stage* in order to develop a picture of the 'whole child'. However, the Foundation Stage Profile captures the Early Learning Goals as a set of thirteen assessment scales, each of which has nine points and will specifically be used to report to parents, Key Stage 1 teachers and the LEA.

Assessment of your learning needs

How far have you developed your understanding of assessing and recording children's learning? Reflect on the needs analysis table below and if possible discuss your ideas and your evidence with a colleague, teacher or tutor.

Making sense of the context	Date/evidence	Making a contribution to the setting	Date/evidence	Taking greater responsibility for or within the setting	Date/evidence
I am aware of the necessity for observing and listening to children to find out about their understanding and achievements.		I have read, discussed with a practitioner and now understand the setting/school policy on assessment and record keeping.		I am aware of and have some experience of the statutory requirements for assessing, recording and reporting in the Foundation Stage.	
I have observed the ways in which practitioners recognise and acknowledge children's achievements.		I can involve children in assessing their own learning and incorporate this into my practice.		I can involve parents in their child's learning on an ongoing basis and recognise the need for effective communication with parents.	
I can observe and listen to individual children in order to assess them.		I can select, plan for and use a range of observation strategies in my teaching for individuals and groups of children.		I recognise the need to keep ongoing records on children's development and learning and can do this.	
I understand the need to use different forms of observation for different purposes. I am aware of the challenges of different forms of observation.		I can plan for and involve other adults in observing and assessing children.		I understand the need to continually monitor and evaluate the nature of the provision available for children in the Foundation Stage.	
I understand and know how to use my observations to begin to make interpretations about children's development and learning.		I understand how to use assessment information to inform my future planning for individuals, groups and a class.		I can annotate and record children's progress and achievements using Stepping Stones and Early Learning Goals.	
I am beginning to understand how to use my interpretations to take children's development and learning forward.		I understand the relationship between assessment and planning and can use this in my teaching.		I can use a range of observation schedules and evidence to evaluate all aspects of the provision in the setting in which I am working.	
If one or more of these is not yet ticked, you may find it helpful to complete the activities on **pages 60 to 64.**		If one or more of these is not yet ticked, you may find it helpful to complete the activities on **pages 91 to 95.**		If one or more of these is not yet ticked, you may find it helpful to complete the activities on **pages 116 to 120.**	

Chapter 2   Guidance and needs analysis

Conclusion

This chapter has introduced you to some aspects of Foundation Stage practice, which you need to know and understand in order to become an effective early years practitioner. Having read this chapter and completed the needs analysis you should be more aware of your strengths and areas in need of further development. At the end of each needs analysis column are page references that will help you plan your learning for each theme discussed in Chapters 3, 4 and 5. Make sure you discuss your training or learning needs, based on what you have learned from completing this chapter, with your training provider or lead practitioner.

Chapter 3　Making sense of the context
ᴐ Introduction

Contents

Introduction

The information and activities in this section are aimed at practitioners who are in the early stages of working in a Foundation Stage setting. This may include undergraduates studying early childhood education, trainee teachers beginning their training as Foundation Stage practitioners, or teachers who are already qualified and who wish to change phases to work in the Foundation Stage. The activities described can be carried out in any Foundation Stage setting, and across the areas of learning outlined in the *Curriculum Guidance*. Foundation Stage settings are complex places and this chapter is designed to support you as you begin to get to know, and make sense of practice in the setting.

The *Curriculum Guidance for the Foundation Stage* identifies a number of principles which are '*drawn from, and are evident in, good and effective practice in early years settings*' (QCA, 2000 page11). A summary of this book's coverage of the principles included in the *Curriculum Guidance* is given in an Appendix at the end of the book. It may be helpful to you to refer to this.

If you are training to be a teacher in the Foundation Stage you will need to audit your development by reference to the statements in *Qualifying to Teach Professional Standards for Qualified Teacher Status* (DfES/TTA, 2003), which set out what a trainee teacher must know, understand and be able to do to be awarded QTS. A summary of the Standards that are addressed by different themes is also included as an Appendix. Please refer to this regularly.

As you complete each piece of evidence that accompanies the activities it is important that you share this with your supervising practitioner, school based mentor, colleagues and/or tutor, as relevant to your situation. This profiling process is particularly important for trainee teachers, and your training provider should advise you on this. Do ensure that you link the completion of the activities in this chapter with the profiling requirements of your training.

The matrix below outlines the content and activities for this chapter. Use it to help you plan your further learning. If you are a trainee teacher use the summary of the Standards for the Award of Teacher Status to see how your experiences at this level can contribute directly to the profiling process.

	When finding out about policy and practice in the setting	When observing children	When observing other practitioners	When evaluating planning, or planning an activity or lesson	When reflecting on your practice
Young children as learners and enquirers	Read the early years policy and discuss it with the lead practitioner. Identify the theoretical basis for activities children undertake.	Observe how children use their senses to engage actively in learning.	Observe how adults interact with children and how children are supported by this interaction.		Reflect on the effectiveness of the approaches adopted.
Making connections in children's learning	Become familiar with the features of play.	Observe children playing and analyse this using your understanding of the features of play.			Reflect on your understanding of play and the features that enable or hinder the development of high quality play.
Adults and children working together	Become familiar with the basic information about the organisation of the setting. Identify the roles and responsibilities of adults in the setting.	Observe children's interactions with other children in a range of contexts.			Reflect on what you can learn about children from observation, and how you might support children to develop respectful relationships with others.
Organising the environment for learning	Become familiar with the indicators of a successful working environment.	Observe, analyse and evaluate children's use of the environment. Observe children using resources and evaluate the appropriateness of these.		Plan one or more activities with another member of the team, focusing on the provision of resources.	Evaluate children's use of the environment and its resources and reflect on the changes you would make in the light of these evaluations.
Planning for learning	Be aware of the philosophical or methodological principles underpinning planning in the setting. Explore these with the lead practitioner.			Analyse the planning of three activities to identify coverage of the areas of learning.	Evaluate planning and identify and changes that you might wish to see made.
Observing and assessing young children	Understand the issues related to confidentiality and adhere to this principle.	Using an observation schedule to observe a child. Use this information to identify what you can learn about the child and about the process of observation.			Interpret observations and reflect on how information from observation can help you plan for a child's learning or development.

All the activities in this chapter are outlined in full and have the following information provided with them:

⊃ essential background to the activity, including the use of resources and which context might be the most appropriate for carrying it out;
⊃ suggested background reading (if relevant);
⊃ a description of the activity and all the elements that go to make it up;
⊃ ideas on how to evaluate its success;
⊃ your achievements.

Chapter 3 Young children as learners and enquirers

Putting theory into practice

One of the principles in the *Curriculum Guidance for the Foundation Stage* (QCA, 2000) states that *'effective learning and development for young children requires high-quality care and education by practitioners'* (page 12). This can only be achieved by practitioners having a clear understanding of the theoretical underpinning on which early years practice is based. From your reading of Chapter 2 and referring to the additional readings detailed in the chapter you should now have a foundation upon which to base your own growing knowledge and understanding. You now need to make links between theory and practice.

As the DfEE (1990) has stated, all early years settings should have a policy outlining their aims and objectives for children. This policy should encompass beliefs on how children develop and learn and how the practitioners in the setting will facilitate this. These beliefs may be embedded within an overall early years policy or there may be a specific policy on learning and teaching. This policy should be based on a clear philosophy and shared by practitioners and parents.

Active learning and first-hand experiences

According to QCA (2000) children learn through movement and using all their senses. This is a key aspect in young children's learning. Children use their senses to understand and build up their knowledge of concepts and ideas. As Fisher (2002) states: *'being active means that the young child engages with experiences, actively (as opposed to passively) bringing his or her existing knowledge to bear on what is currently under investigation'* (page 12). Without this crucial experience, children are unable to engage in meaningful learning.

Preparation
Read the early years policy and, if possible, read Bruce (1997) Chapter 3.

Set aside some time to have a discussion with the lead practitioner. Agree some observation time with the team so that you can begin to make links between learning theories and classroom practice.

Task
1   Using the early years policy as a starting point, discuss with the lead practitioner, their ideas and your ideas about the theoretical influences on their practice and work with young children. Write up your discussion.
2   Observe a range of activities and learning situations during the week. Begin to identify the theoretical basis for each activity or situation using Bruce (1997) Chapter 3 for reference.
3   Also note how the children are using their senses to engage in active learning and record what they say.
4   Use the table below to help structure your observations.

Activity/situation	What is happening?	What is the theoretical basis?

Evaluation and follow up

In your evaluation consider the following questions:

- ➲ What learning did the children engage in?
- ➲ Which senses did the children use?
- ➲ How did they comment upon their experience?
- ➲ How does the learning and teaching relate to the ideas discussed with the lead practitioner?
- ➲ What is the theoretical underpinning for the activities/learning situations that you have observed?
- ➲ Are different theoretical approaches used for different activities/situations?
- ➲ Which theoretical approaches underpin activities, which seem successful?
- ➲ Do you consider any of the approaches to be used inappropriately?

Child development

Two recent research projects looking at effective pedagogy (Moyles *et al.*, 2002 and Siraj-Blatchford *et al.*, 2002) both identify the importance of practitioners having in-depth knowledge and understanding of how children develop and that this is linked to positive outcomes for young children. A good resource to illustrate norms and sequences of development is Sheridan (1997), *From Birth to Five Years*.

It is important to remember when looking at children's development that although different areas of development are identified the child must be seen as a whole being and that one area of development is not more important than another. It is also vital to remember that one area of development can impact upon another.

Example: *Due to problems at birth Cain has gross motor difficulties. He lacks co-ordination when running, jumping or climbing and at times can fall over. Consequently he does not like to go outside or join in activities involving the use of these skills. Cain also lacks confidence within group situations and is unwilling to participate and socialise with the other children. This results in delayed social skills.*

In addition, it is also important to contextualise the child. Social and cultural influences can promote or hinder a child's development.

Example: *Pascal has well developed language skills. He has a large vocabulary and uses sophisticated sentence structure. He asks many questions and is interested in how others speak and the language they use. Since birth Pascal has had the undivided attention of many adults and has always been spoken and listened to with care and affection, his questions answered and his opinions taken seriously.*

Children feeling safe and secure

QCA (2000) states that children need to feel safe and secure in order to become effective and confident learners. In part this is achieved through working with parents and building up a sense of trust between all parties involved in the learning and education process. This is discussed more fully in the theme 'Adults and children working together' (**pages 14–16**). In addition, adults working with young children need to treat them with respect and listen to them. If children know that they will be heard and given attention they will then have a secure foundation from which to grow in confidence and take risks in their learning (Edgington, 1998).

Preparation

Agree an observation time with the team so that you can observe and make links between how adults interact with children and children feeling safe and secure. How children interact with each other is discussed on **page 51**.

Task

Observe adults and children interacting. Note how adults respond to children and how they encourage them to learn. This may be verbal through encouragement and praise or it may be non-verbal through signalling gestures such as with thumbs up or smiling. Note the children's response to this. Use the following table to structure your observation and note taking.

Initial comments. By whom?	Response. By whom?	Further comments/response. By whom?	Outcome

Evaluation and follow up

Reflect and evaluate your observation using the following questions:

- ➲ Do adults employ a range of verbal and non-verbal strategies for interacting with children?
- ➲ What positive language is employed to help children feel confident?
- ➲ How did the children respond to positive adult interaction?
- ➲ Are children encouraged to return to adults for additional help?
- ➲ Generally, are children confident in the setting?
- ➲ How are less confident children managed?
- ➲ Were all children encouraged in their work?
- ➲ If there were instances of children not being encouraged how did they respond to this?

Your achievements

Now you have read this section and completed the activities you should be able to:

- ➲ recognise the different theoretical approaches that underpin early years practice;
- ➲ identify the theoretical basis for different activities/classroom situations;
- ➲ recognise the implications of different theories for your own practice;
- ➲ understand the importance of having knowledge of child development;
- ➲ identify some of the influences on a child's development;
- ➲ identify what constitutes effective first-hand experiences for children which involve them in active learning;
- ➲ identify communication strategies which enable children to feel safe and secure;
- ➲ use positive language with children which help them to feel trust and to be confident with you.

If you feel that you have completed the tasks successfully, return to the relevant needs analysis and mark it off with the date and evidence. If appropriate, ask your tutor about being able to use this as evidence of your understanding or professional capability. This information could be used as part of the course you are studying. This may be evidence towards the Professional Standards for QTS or it might be part of a profile or an assignment you might be completing as part of your studies. Please refer to the tables at the back of the book which detail coverage against the principles listed within the *Curriculum Guidance for the Foundation Stage* as well as the Professional Standards for QTS.

Chapter 3   Making connections in children's learning

Quality play

In the previous chapter you were introduced to the complex nature of defining play. You were also introduced to types of play and how ultimately play must be seen as a process. For a discussion of this read Moyles (1989, Chapter 1). Whilst considering types of play is useful in highlighting the value of and range of play activities children engage in, some play theorists have preferred to concentrate on the process of play and identifying the characteristics of quality play.

Bruce (1991) proposed the idea of 'free-flow play' and identified possible indicators for quality play especially free-flow play. From her original work Bruce (2001, page 30) has developed twelve features of quality play and advises that for children to be engaged in high quality play many or most of these features should be present. The twelve features of play are:

1   Children use the first-hand experiences that they have in life.
2   Children make up rules as they play, and so keep control of their play.
3   Children make play props.
4   Children choose to play. They cannot be made to play.
5   Children rehearse the future in their role-play.
6   Children pretend when they play.
7   Children play alone sometimes.
8   Children and/or adults play together, in parallel, associatively, or co-operatively in pairs or groups.
9   Each player has a personal play agenda, although they may not be aware of this.
10   Children playing will be deeply involved, and difficult to distract from their deep learning. Children at play wallow in their learning.
11   Children try out their most recent learning, skills and competencies when they play. They seem to celebrate what they know.
12   Children at play co-ordinate their ideas, feelings and make sense of relationships with their family, friends and culture. When play is co-ordinated it flows along in a sustained way. It is called free-flow play.

Preparation
Familiarise yourself with the above twelve features of play.

Prepare to observe children at play.

Discuss with your practitioner their ideas about high quality play and how they cater for it in the setting.

Task
Over a week carry out a series of five-minute observations of four children playing in different areas of the setting. Record your observations. Use the following table to analyse your observations against the twelve features of play. You will need a table for each child. Share your observations with the practitioner.

Child 1	Activity 1	Activity 2	Activity 3	Activity 4
Feature 1				
Feature 2				
Feature 3				
Feature 4				
Feature 5				
Feature 6				
Feature 7				
Feature 8				
Feature 9				
Feature 10				
Feature 11				
Feature 12				

Evaluation and follow up

Reflect on and evaluate your observations using the following questions:

➲ How many of the features were present?
➲ Why were some features absent?
➲ What enabled the children to engage in high quality play?
➲ What hindered the development of high quality play?
➲ Were some features easier to distinguish than others?
➲ What, if any, were the drawbacks to using this tool to identify high quality play?
➲ Through your observations and discussion what is your own understanding of high quality play?

Play and creativity

Play and creativity are clearly linked. Through play children can create new worlds, use their imaginations and think in flexible and novel ways. In doing this children engage in a creative process, which enables them to progress in their development and learning. According to Duffy (1998, page 81), a model of the creative process has four levels. These are:

1 Curiosity – what is it?
2 Exploration – what can it do? What does it do?
3 Play – what can I do with this?
4 Creativity – what can I create or invent from this?

Children do not progress through this process in a linear way but move backwards and forwards through this process as they progress in their learning.

Language and communication

The role of talk

Talking is a shared means of communication and can include sign language. Talking is crucial for young children's development and learning because it:

➲ enables them to play with others and socialise;
➲ enables them to make connections and extend their learning;
➲ provides the foundation for literacy;
➲ gives adults a window into the child's thinking and growing understanding. This in turn aids both planning and assessment (adapted from Edgington, 1998).

It is thought that many children when entering the Foundation Stage have poorly developed language skills (Basic Skills Agency, 2002) and so developing language through talking with children must be a priority. QCA (2000) states that *'a major role in teaching involves extending children's language sensitively, while acknowledging and showing respect for home language, local dialect and any forms of augmentative communication that children may be using'* (page 23). In order to extend children's language it is important to have an understanding of how children's language develops. Please remember that children develop in different ways and that the timetable that follows is simply a guide.

Language development
A timetable of language development:

Approximate age	Features of language
6 months	Babbles.
1 year	Knows own name and some other words. First word.
18 months	Select an object on request, follow simple commands, variety of single word utterances.
2 years	Follows commands containing two key ideas, using two word phrases – telegrammatic speech.
2.5 years	Identify objects by use, enjoys simple stories, using 3–4 word phrases, beginning to use past tense.
3 years	Understands longer/more complex sentences, beginning to understand negatives and plurals, using 3–5 word sentences, over-generalisation of grammatical rules.
4 years	Follows instructions with 3 verbal concepts, using sentences of 4–5 words, asking lots of questions
5 years	Understands most everyday conversations, beginning to understand jokes, using 5+ word sentences, relate simple stories, uses past, present and future tense.

(Adapted from Gale *et al.*, 1995)

Your achievements

Now you have read this section and completed the activities you should be able to:

➲ recognise the twelve features of play;
➲ link theoretical understanding of play to practice;
➲ link theoretical understanding of the creative process to practice;
➲ make connections between play and creativity;
➲ understand the importance of talk in young children's development;
➲ understand the importance of appropriate adult interaction in developing children's language.

If you feel that you have completed the tasks successfully, return to the relevant needs analysis and mark it off with the date and evidence. If appropriate, ask your tutor about being able to use this as evidence of your understanding or professional capability. This information could be used as part of the course you are studying. This may be evidence towards the Professional Standards for QTS or it might be part of a profile or an assignment you might be completing as part of your studies. Please refer to the tables at the back of the book which detail coverage against the principles listed within the *Curriculum Guidance for the Foundation Stage* as well as the Professional Standards for QTS.

Chapter 3 — Adults and children working together

In this section you will begin to gather information about the setting in which you are placed. It is important that you get to know the nature of the setting and its children, focusing in particular on the relationships between children themselves and between children and adults.

If this is your first experience of a nursery or Reception class you may feel completely overwhelmed by all that is going on around you. Don't panic. Be sensitive and observant, listen, ask questions and enjoy the experience. Gradually the pieces of the puzzle will fit together.

In the handbook for the setting, there will be a range of information about all aspects of life in the setting. At present you will focus on:

➲ staff;
➲ children's safety, well-being, importance of gathering information from parents about children's allergies, medical conditions, dietary requirements;
➲ procedures to follow if a child is ill or has an accident;
➲ having respect for and getting to know each child and what he or she brings in the way of personality, experience, knowledge and skills;
➲ recognition and respect for differences in individuals, families, ethnicity, religion, food, cultural practices and festivals.

There will be a great deal of information about your setting which you will assimilate gradually as you talk to the staff and become experienced.

Staff within the setting

In the setting you will meet a number of colleagues who will have different roles and responsibilities. It is essential for the success of the setting and the well-being of the children that these staff work together effectively.

The team may include the head teacher who, in a small infant or primary school, or in a nursery school may be a teaching head who also has overall responsibility for the running of the school; class teacher(s), nursery nurses, classroom assistants and bilingual assistants (who support children, parents and carers whose first language is not English).

Other staff such as office staff, caretakers, cleaners, cooks and lunchtime supervisors as well as crossing patrol staff may all contribute in different ways. Although the children will not have regular contact with these people, they often add an extra dimension to life in the setting.

Settings that offer placements to trainees and students generally do so out of a wish to support and develop the staff of the future and will work hard to ensure that you are made welcome and supported. You in turn must respond sensitively to your colleagues and recognise their wealth of experience. Take time to observe how they respond to the children and to each other. Courteous and respectful relationships are essential to the ethos of the setting.

Preparation

Identify the immediate members of the team and check that they are willing to discuss their roles and responsibilities. Think about the questions you will need to ask them and make a list of these. Your questions should elicit information about their role and responsibilities, and how they see these in relation to the team as a whole.

Task

Find time to speak with each person, ensuring that you meet in a place and at a time that shows your colleagues that you value the opportunity to discuss this with them.

Evaluation and follow up

Reflect on and summarise your discussions with your colleagues. Think about how your developing understanding of the complex roles and responsibilities will influence your contribution to the work of the setting. Discuss this with the lead practitioner.

As a Foundation Stage practitioner you may be responsible for leading and managing the work of the early years team, which is a complex and challenging role. This is discussed in more detail in Chapter 5, **page 106**.

Adults relating to and respecting children

In your class there may be children whose religion, culture or family preference prevent them from eating certain foods or taking part in some activities. If there are aspects of the religions and cultures of the children that baffle you, ask for an explanation, but remember that the staff around you are probably very experienced and have taken many years, in dialogue with members of families and the community, to acquire their huge body of knowledge and their expertise.

Example: *In the nursery, they are planning a shared picnic. Everyone is going to bring some food. Benjamin is a Rastafarian, Emil is a vegetarian and Shahana is a Muslim. Daisy brings some ham sandwiches as her contribution. All the staff and students are aware of those who may not eat them. It is the custom in the nursery that food which cannot be eaten by everyone is not put on the tables for children to help themselves but handed around by the staff, thus ensuring that no-one eats any forbidden food.*

It would be helpful for you to read the chapter by Tacagni in Smidt, (1998). In this, she describes a project on food and the way in which individual racial and cultural differences were acknowledged and celebrated. It is essential to your practice that you seek ways of encouraging children to recognise and celebrate diversity and the individuality of others, with respect.

Example: *The families of the Muslim children in the Reception class are celebrating Eid ul Fitr. When this is discussed in class, parallels are drawn with Christmas, Easter and Chinese New Year. The Eid party is an annual event in the school calendar. Parents are asked to contribute food and children wear their party clothes. For the Muslim children, these are the special clothes bought for them to celebrate Eid.*

It is vital that you get to know the children well, as soon as possible. This includes accuracy when pronouncing and spelling names, understanding their family background, culture, faith, home language/s as well as any particular medical conditions or special needs. Ensure that you are aware of this information in your class.

Supporting children to develop respectful relationships

When children join an early years setting, this may be the first time they encounter children outside their own family or social circle. They may lack confidence to communicate with others. It is vital that the staff model respectful and friendly approaches and behaviour towards others so that children develop positive attitudes.

Children relate to others in different ways. Some are confident and outgoing; some are confident but do not appear to need a lot of contact with others. Some children choose to play and chat together whilst others are happy to observe, and are clearly engaged in the situation although not taking an active part.

It is important that you create opportunities to observe children's interactions with one another. This will tell you a great deal about them and their relationships with others.

Preparation
In discussion with the lead practitioner identify three children to observe. Plan opportunities to observe them in different situations, for example: outdoors, in the role-play area, when sharing books or when playing with sand or water.

Task
Using the pro forma below, make observations on the child's interactions with other children.

Name of child	Play activity	Other children involved	Nature of interaction

Evaluation and follow up
Reflect on your observations. You could ask yourself the following questions:

➲ Have I learned more about the child?
➲ What was the nature of his or her interaction with others?
➲ Did any of the interactions surprise me?
➲ Did the child interact with a range of others or with the same few?
➲ Do I need to support the child to develop relationships? If so, how will I do this?

Discuss this with your colleagues.

Your achievements

Now you have read this section and completed the activities you should be able to:

⊃ identify the different staff members within the setting;
⊃ clarify the roles and responsibilities of different members of staff;
⊃ gather information about the children as individuals;
⊃ recognise the need to be aware of all the different information available about individual children and the implications for this;
⊃ support children in developing respectful relationships with one another and the adults within the setting;
⊃ use information from your observations to find out about how the children are interacting with one another and the nature of these interactions;
⊃ use your observations to find out about what play activities the children are engaged in and how they are responding within the different parts of the learning environment.

If you feel that you have completed the tasks successfully, return to the relevant needs analysis and mark it off with the date and evidence. If appropriate, ask your tutor about being able to use this as evidence of your understanding or professional capability. This information could be used as part of the course you are studying. This may be evidence towards the Professional Standards for QTS or it might be part of a profile or an assignment you might be completing as part of your studies. Please refer to the tables at the back of the book which detail coverage against the principles listed within the *Curriculum Guidance for the Foundation Stage* as well as the Professional Standards for QTS.

Chapter 3   Organising the environment for learning

Observation and evaluation

In Chapter 2 you were introduced to reasons for providing a well-planned learning environment and to some of the influences that help to shape particular environments. The environmental theme continues with a focus on the way in which the learning environment is used by adults and children.

Successful organisation and use of space will reflect positive relationships between adults and children and will have a very important and lasting effect on children's willingness and motivation to learn. Asprey *et al.* (2002) suggest that older children should be involved in choosing classroom routines. Very young children can also become a part of this process and should be included in decision-making and reflecting on the way in which their learning environment could work better for them. An environment should be continually evolving to support independence and allow children to manage resources and routines for sustained learning. Below are some of the visible indicators of a successful working environment:

➲ adults and children sharing what is important to them in order to develop mutual respect and understanding;
➲ children engaged in relevant learning experiences that encourage curiosity, exploration and independence;
➲ continual dialogue between adults and children where listening, time to communicate and respect for each other are apparent;
➲ negotiation between adults and children to establish the ground rules for joint needs in the particular setting;
➲ physical space and general organisation and management that encourages relaxed yet purposeful opportunities for learning;
➲ sensitive observation and monitoring of the environment to ensure that it is organised to support all children's learning;
➲ displays that celebrate children's achievements and communicate something of the classroom ethos.

Young children need a voice and this means time to be heard and patience on the part of adults to allow them to make their meaning clear. They need to be able to make sense of their environment and understand how it relates to their current view of themselves as learners. The environment should reflect local culture and values as well as national aspirations and international perspectives. Take time to observe and reflect on your environment and if possible visit other settings. Each physical space has unique constraints (Moyles 1995) and the opportunities for successful play and opportunities for active learning will be supported in different ways.

Observation is an important strategy for monitoring teaching and learning. While becoming familiar with the way that adults and children use the environment carry out structured observation followed by analysis. Evidence from these tasks will be referred to again in Chapter 5 of this theme (**pages 109 to 111**).

Preparation

If possible, read Fisher (2002a, Chapter 8). She considers key issues such as the use of space, provision of resources, involving children in decision making and establishing independence.

Task

⮞ Observe carefully in the indoor or the outdoor space.

⮞ Choose a defined area and use the observation sheet below to record your findings over one week. Repeat the observations in the same area at different times during the week to gain a comprehensive picture.

⮞ Repeat the same type of observation in all the main areas of the classroom to gain a holistic view of the use of the learning environment.

Domestic play area	10 minute observation
How many children used the area?	
What were the children doing?	
Was there an imbalance between boys and girls? If so why?	
How long did the children stay in the area?	
Describe the resources used by the children and how they were used?	
What was the role of adults?	

Analyse your observations from a range of areas using the following questions as a framework:

⮞ Which areas provide children with the most satisfying experiences?

⮞ Which areas are used in an unacceptable, purposeless way?

⮞ Can you give examples of children showing a high level of involvement/concentration?

⮞ What resources are best used?

⮞ How would you describe the role of adults?

Below are sample observations from four areas.

Area	Type of use	Possible reasons
1 Domestic play area	Used frequently and imaginatively but only by girls.	No artefacts for boys to relate to easily. Active rejection of boys by girls – no adult intervention.
2 Book area	Not used during three 10-minute observation times.	Books in very poor condition, cushions dirty and no adult encouragement.
3 Table top area	Used by boys and girls – mainly for teacher directed activities such as writing and recording numeracy tasks.	Overemphasis on control of activities by adults with little regard for interests of the children.
4 Outdoor play area – hard surface	Used by boys – mainly riding bikes and kicking balls.	No space set aside for quieter or more creative play – no adult involvement in the children's play.

As you observe the majority of learning areas you should begin to understand the pattern of children's use of the environment and reflect on possible changes that could be made in the short term and in the longer term. Take time to talk to children about their preferences.

Evaluation and follow up

Following the observations, the need for change may be obvious. How and when to make the changes will be a matter for negotiation between adults and children. The next task continues this theme.

Resources

Resources, either commercial or improvised, are intended to support and extend children's learning. It is important to audit resources and to decide which ones contribute to learning, how they should be organised and accessed, and how decisions are made about replenishing resources on either a short-term or long-term basis. The following task focuses on organisation and accessibility of resources and their relevance for the children and the task.

Following on from the observation of the learning environment you need to consider the part played by

Preparation

Following on from the observation of the learning environment you need to consider the part played by resources. Watch the organisation and management of a morning or an afternoon session and look at the resources used in child initiated and adult lead activities. Remember that the most successful environments are those that are flexible, with resources used to represent a myriad of possibilities and with learning areas that are interchangeable. As Asprey *et al.* (2002, page 51) say, *'The rhythm of … each day should provide opportunities for children to learn in different ways'.*

Task

Share the planning for several learning situations with another team member. Describe the resources you intend to use and list them on a planning sheet that also identifies outcomes for children's learning and an evaluation of the session.

Evaluation and follow up

Having used the resources consider the following questions:

- How well did the resources relate to the tasks?
- Were the children encouraged to select resources and to use them independently?
- Did you find problems with the resources? If so, what were they?
- Which resources would you discard?

Displays

Displays determine the way the classroom looks and they make a distinct impression on children and adults. Williams (2003, pages 78 to 79) suggests that teachers should 'stop, look and listen'. She poses questions:

- What purposes are served by displays?
- Could displays make a more efficient and realistic contribution to learning?
- Is there an approach to display that will provide a more sensitive, interactive and informative advertisement for the whole curriculum?
- How can displays reflect the cultural experience of children?
- Who decides what will be displayed?
- How can children be given encouragement to make independent displays that include aspects of life outside school?
- Do we understand that not everybody will appreciate a particular style of display?
- How much time is spent on the organisation of displays? Is this time well spent?

Independence

Teachers need to appreciate the range of attitudes and experience that children bring with them to Foundation Stage settings and to provide a climate in which they can reach their potential and where an increase in independence as well as collective responsibility is valued. An independent approach will also have benefits for teachers.

You have now had the opportunity to observe and evaluate the way in which children use the environment. The tasks are ones that practitioners often mean to carry out but fail to accomplish through a lack of time or inclination. The time will no longer be spent on 'housekeeping' and making decisions for children but on quality interaction with other children where it may be needed most.

Your achievements

Now that you have read this section and completed the activities you should be able to:

- recognise indicators of a successful working environment;
- observe and analyse children's use of the environment;
- make changes to the environment based on evidence from observation;
- carry out an audit of resources;
- evaluate the appropriateness and value of resources to support and extend children's learning;
- understand how the environment can support children's independence;
- understand the purpose of display and the importance of a shared approach.

C3 Environment for learning

If you feel that you have completed the tasks successfully, return to the relevant needs analysis and mark it off with the date and evidence. If appropriate, ask your tutor about being able to use this as evidence of your understanding or professional capability. This information could be used as part of the course you are studying. This may be evidence towards the Professional Standards for QTS or it might be part of a profile or an assignment you might be completing as part of your studies. Please refer to the tables at the back of the book which detail coverage against the principles listed within the *Curriculum Guidance for the Foundation Stage* as well as the Professional Standards for QTS.

Chapter 3   Planning for learning

Chapter 2 identified a number of key issues that should be considered when planning for children in the Foundation Stage. In this section you will begin to develop an understanding of the planning process in your setting. You will be asked to explore the theoretical or philosophical approach that informs the learning in the setting or classroom in which you are working.

Different philosophical approaches and planning

Over the past few decades, our education system has to some extent been influenced by different theoretical approaches to early years education such as Steiner, Montessori, High Scope and Reggio Emilia. Some approaches are more prominent in some parts of the UK than others. It is difficult to summarise these contrasting approaches in a few words, but they have all influenced provision and therefore planning approaches in different ways.

Steiner schools, based on the work of Rudolph Steiner (1861–1925) do not begin formal teaching until the year the child is seven. The curriculum is strongly influenced by exploration of the natural world and the elements, the rhythm of the seasons, songs and the arts. Play is central to the curriculum and is valued as a medium for developing concentration and perseverance. The adults in the setting act as mentors who help develop children's creativity and individuality.

In a Montessori setting (Maria Montessori, 1870–1952) the emphasis is on creating the right environment in which the developing child can have a structure within which to think and learn independently. There is considerable emphasis on providing materials which are deemed appropriate and which are used in specific ways to sustain and develop the child's natural *self-creating energies'* (Montessori, 1965). There is an emphasis on 'practical life' experience, using scaled down versions of real domestic equipment. The curriculum reflects a focus on the intellectual, through practical activity, education through the senses, language and maths. The cultural curriculum of geography, history, biology, music and the arts overlays this (Miller, *et al.* 2003). The practitioners in the setting are regarded as guides to children's learning rather than as teachers.

High Scope, which originated in the United States, is highly structured. Based on a rigorous early intervention strategy it has been evaluated in a number of research projects. The High Scope approach requires children to 'plan, do and review' their activities. It encourages children to assume responsibility for their own experience in the setting or classroom. Time is allowed each day for children to plan their activities and record these in some format. Proponents of this approach argue that it supports the development of autonomy, commitment and aspirations to be learners in children. For more on the evaluation of High Scope and other early intervention approaches, see Pugh (2002).

In the pre-schools of Reggio Emilia, the term 'the hundred languages of children' is used to describe the variety and richness of children's expression in all its forms. The Reggio Emilia pedagogy is based on the notion of 'reciprocal learning'. Learning is a shared experience, promoting dialogue and questioning based on an experiential, responsive and developmental approach to teaching and learning. Projects often arise and develop through the interests of the children.

All of these philosophies, with their particular view of the education of young children, have influenced educational thinking in the UK. The organisation, curriculum and therefore the planning in nursery and Reception classes may reflect some of these approaches. Further information about these approaches can be obtained from texts listed in the bibliography on **pages 26 to 27**.

Preparation

Talk to the nursery or Reception teacher about the nature of the setting or school. Explore the philosophical or methodological principles that underpin the provision. To do this you may need to plan the questions you will ask. These might include questions such as:

- Is there one particular approach that is used in the nursery/class?
- What approach to learning and teaching is used here?
- How do you plan the curriculum?
- What principles do you follow when you plan the activities you offer children?
- What aspects of learning are most important to you when you plan for the children?

You may need to devise additional questions which relate to the setting in which you are working. You could explore why certain approaches are adopted and whether these philosophical approaches are shared between all staff. The importance of developing a shared philosophy and policy on teaching and learning is explored in greater detail in Chapter 5, **page 99**.

Task

Re-read the role-play example and the analysis of Rosie's play in Chapter 2, **pages 23 and 24**. Ask your teacher or mentor for a copy of the planning for the class or children you will be working with. Look at three planned activities. Using the Curriculum Guidance for the Foundation Stage, decide which areas of learning they may have been planned to address, or could reflect. Use the table below to identify the areas of learning that the activity addresses.

Activity	Children involved (if appropriate)
Area of learning	Learning objectives from the Stepping Stones or Early Learning Goals
Personal, social and emotional development	
Communication, language and literacy	
Mathematical development	
Knowledge and understanding of the world	
Physical development	
Creative development	

Evaluation and follow up

Evaluate the activities in terms of the areas of learning covered. Are there any gaps? Using this information, should there be changes to the planning to offer children the opportunity to experience all of the areas of learning?

Your achievements

Now that you have read this section and completed the activities you should be able to:

◐ recognise that planning must reflect the way that children learn;
◐ recognise that planning must be based on the areas of learning of the Foundation Stage guidance;
◐ understand that planned activities should be challenging and matched to the needs of the child;
◐ recognise that there are different philosophical approaches underpinning early years education, which influence planning;
◐ recognise the philosophical view or views which determines the planning approach in your setting;
◐ analyse and evaluate the planning in your setting to identify the areas of learning covered.

If you feel that you have completed the tasks successfully, return to the relevant needs analysis and mark it off with the date and evidence. If appropriate, ask your tutor about being able to use this as evidence of your understanding or professional capability. This information could be used as part of the course you are studying. This may be evidence towards the Professional Standards for QTS or it might be part of a profile or an assignment you might be completing as part of your studies. Please refer to the tables at the back of the book which detail coverage against the principles listed within the *Curriculum Guidance for the Foundation Stage* as well as the Professional Standards for QTS.

Chapter 3 Observing and assessing young children

What is formative assessment?

'Formative assessment involves the piecing together of planned and incidental assessments to plan and provide for the successful learning of each child.'

(Ebbutt, 1996, page 143)

Throughout the Foundation Stage (and beyond) practitioners will want to gain accurate information about how children are developing and learning in relation to their knowledge, understanding and skills as well as their disposition towards and attitudes about themselves as learners. This information enables practitioners to monitor children's progress and also to evaluate the quality of the provision offered to them, including the curriculum available. For example, are all children given equal access to your time and attention or to the curriculum? These are important questions for practitioners to ask themselves on a regular basis. We can use this information to identify strengths as well as areas of weakness in the curriculum we provide for all children. This can be an important source of evidence within the current context of high levels of accountability to parents, colleagues and other professionals.

Practitioners are bound to use intuitive judgements about children gained through their daily interactions with them at work and play. However, evidence gathered should be used to refine these judgements and support intuitive views. This is essential given the research findings, which link teacher expectations to children's performance. This suggests that children who the teacher expects to do well generally do perform better whilst those children for whom the teacher does not have such high expectations perform less well. This process of gathering information can produce some unexpected results, which might surprise the practitioner. It can also serve to increase the rigour with which a practitioner investigates the boundaries of a child's learning. This is helpful both when a child is causing concern and for a very high attaining child.

What strategies should I be using to gather formative assessment evidence?

A number of formative assessment strategies can be used to gather evidence of children's learning at play and at work and you will need to become proficient in using these within your own teaching. However within this chapter we are going to consider only the use of observation and listening since these are fundamental to the work of early years practitioners.

Observation

Observations are used to gather evidence of children's 'meaning-making' of the environment around them including people and resources within that context. It is for this reason that the richest kind of evidence comes often from observations of children at play, when they are in control of the activity and free to interpret what they do. Generally in these situations the children have more responsibility for their own learning and are able to make their own decisions about what they do and how they do it.

There are different types of observation. At one end of the continuum the teacher should simply observe, without intervening or interrupting in any way. This means avoiding eye contact, conversation, or any form of interaction as far as possible. On other occasions it may be important to carry out targeted observations, which is a more specific form of enquiry. These kinds of observations are usually more carefully structured and focused in order to address a particular question the practitioner may have. The question may be related to how children are playing within different areas of the setting or classroom, how they are using particular resources, or even specific questions you may have about individual or small groups of children. For example, you may wish to find out how children are using the large blocks available in one area of your setting. If you discover that very limited use is being made of these, your observations may lead you to support the children in different ways, model new ways of playing or even just add new combinations of play resources alongside the large blocks.

At the other end of the continuum, the teacher may be observing but still participating in some kind of interaction with children. All forms of observation can provide useful information about what children do, how they go about their work and interact with one another. When recording observations it is always important to note something about the context in which the observation took place. However, observation alone might not enable the teacher to gain access to children's thinking or reasoning unless this happens to be apparent. This is why it is very important for teachers to develop the skills of listening and *really* hearing what it is that children are saying to them rather than what they *think* the children are saying.

The challenge of observation
One of the greatest challenges is the need to be objective and unbiased. We must not allow our objectivity to be influenced by preconceived ideas about a child's attainment or any stereotypical notions that might relate to behaviour, home background, ethnic origin or gender. Bias can also be present if you observe with a view to finding particular information and therefore observe selectively or interpret as you observe rather than simply recording the evidence.

Observation can also be a time consuming process. It does need to be carefully organised and managed within the setting or classroom so that everyone is aware of their role and responsibility in relation to observation and assessment. It is essential to involve all those working with children in the observation and assessment process and this needs careful organisation, management and training for all those who are going to be carrying out these processes. Devising ways of integrating observation into practice within a reception class, particularly if there are no additional adults working with you, requires creativity and a commitment to the value of this as an essential tool for your professional practice.

Observation can also be professionally demanding of practitioners. These demands can take the form of being surprised or threatened by the information gathered through observation. When gathering observation data it is also likely that one will be observing the adults working with the children more carefully than usual and this may also engender a sense of fear and anxiety within the adults.

A final challenge to practitioners is that of interpreting or analysing the information that has been gathered. You need to use your understanding of child development along with your professional knowledge to interpret what you see and hear and take a child's learning forward or change your own practice. This is often best achieved through discussions with all those involved in the setting, including nursery nurses, teaching assistants, key workers and other practitioners. A key factor in this process of interpretation is ensuring that the evidence you are working with is gathered objectively and accurately, taking account of the challenges that are identified above. You will have the opportunity to practise this in the second activity below.

Listening
This is an active process and needs to be practised and refined. It is all too easy to offer some kind of comment, question or even non-verbal expression that will interrupt the communication and alter the nature of the interaction taking place. It is easy to forget how much children want to please their teacher and so spend a lot of time and energy trying to work out what it is the teacher wants them to say or do. There is a wealth of literature which indicates that young children are very aware of the power dynamics in a classroom and will alter what they say or do to please an adult because they feel insecure or challenged by an adult (Holt, 1982; Gardner, 1993).

Issues to do with confidentiality

As a trainee teacher or practitioner you need to be aware of issues to do with confidentiality. All written records on individual children need to be recorded using appropriate language so that they are free of judgements and can be shared with parents and carers, as well as other professionals, if required. Try to use specific examples or actual evidence of attainment and avoid making judgements about behaviour, potential ability and so on.

Example: *'Abdul seems to have some difficulties sharing toys with other children and needs support to do this gently.'* **NOT** *'Abdul always snatches toys from other children and behaves spitefully towards them.'*

Preparation
This activity focuses on using an observation schedule. Choose a child to observe on two separate occasions within the setting in which you are working. Devise or copy an observation schedule like the one below on which to record this observation.

Task
Carry out two separate five-minute observations on an individual child at work or play. Ensure that these observations are carried out in different settings and at different times of the day (for example, complete one in the morning and one in the afternoon. Alternatively you may wish to carry out an observation indoors and another outside). Make a record of each observation on a schedule like the one below.

Individual observation sheet	Child
Date	Time
Place	Situation
Observation	
Analysis of your observation	

Evaluation and follow up
Complete the analysis section at the end of the observation.

➲ What have you learned about the process of observation?
➲ What have you learned about this child as a result of each observation?

Evaluate what you have seen and heard in relation to this child. It might help to use the questions below to do this:

➲ Were there any surprises in relation to what this child said or did or how they interacted with their peers?
➲ How involved did the child appear to be in what they were doing?
➲ Why do you think this was?
➲ Is there anything that could have been said or done to improve this level of involvement?
➲ Were there any differences between the two observations? If so, why do you think this was?

Consider what you might want to do with this child next in terms of their development or learning.

Now discuss this with the practitioner responsible for the child.

Interpreting your observations

Preparation and task

Through the activity above you might have discovered that it is quite easy to record what you have seen and heard but considerably more difficult to decide what this tells you about the child or their learning needs, in other words how you might interpret this information. Consider the following examples and record your interpretations. Then consider how you might respond or what action you might take to support each child in their development and learning.

Case study	Interpretation and questions for you to ask	Action
Anya is three years old and loves playing in the water tray. You observe her filling a container and pouring the contents of it time and again into the two other containers available in the water tray. She is laughing while she does it.		
Kedar is three-and-a-half years old and has recently arrived from India. He is not yet speaking any English but you notice that he spends a lot of time in the book corner. When he is in there he takes all the books off the shelves and sorts them out according to their size.		
Marliyo is four years old and loves looking at books. She knows lots of the storybooks by heart and then one day you notice that she is putting her finger under each line of writing as she re-tells the story.		
You observe Imogen wandering around the nursery one day collecting all sorts of things into a little basket that she has found. Before putting each object into her basket she explores it quite carefully, feeling it, turning it over and studying it. Then she puts it into her basket and continues on her way to find more objects. In her basket at the end of this journey are various shells, a paper bag, some small boxes, two nails and some screws of different sizes.		

Evaluation and follow up

You have now had the opportunity to try and interpret some observations and then decide upon what you might do in the light of those interpretations. Our observations do allow us to make guesses about why children play or do things in particular ways, what they already know and what their particular interests might be at this point in their development. However, these are educated guesses based directly upon the evidence but then informed by our own understanding of child development and learning. This process does get easier with practise!

Ask if you can share your interpretations of the scenarios outlined above with other practitioners working in the setting or classroom. Consider the similarities and differences in their views with your own and think about why this might be the case.

It is important to reflect upon what you have discovered about observing and how you might interpret those observations.

Your achievements

Now you have read this section and completed the activities you should be able to:

⊃ understand the nature and purpose of formative assessment;
⊃ employ the strategies of observation and listening in order to gather formative assessment information on individual children;
⊃ recognise the challenges of observation as an assessment tool;
⊃ make some initial interpretations of the evidence you have gathered through your observations;
⊃ understand the issues related to confidentiality.

If you feel that you have completed the tasks successfully, return to the relevant needs analysis and mark it off with the date and evidence. If appropriate, ask your tutor about being able to use this as evidence of your understanding or professional capability. This information could be used as part of the course you are studying. This may be evidence towards the Professional Standards for QTS or it might be part of a profile or an assignment you might be completing as part of your studies. Please refer to the tables at the back of the book which detail coverage against the principles listed within the *Curriculum Guidance for the Foundation Stage* as well as the Professional Standards for QTS.

Conclusion

You have begun to develop your understanding of practice in the Foundation Stage. By the end of this chapter, the combination of your reading and activities in the setting will have helped you understand the complex nature of early years provision. You are now ready to develop your own practice further and make a more substantial contribution to the work of the setting. It is essential that you check you have evidence to support all the statements in the appropriate needs analysis tables for this level. It is also important that you talk to your lead practitioner or school-based mentor at this stage. He or she will be able to help you check that you have appropriate evidence to audit your progress. If you are a trainee teacher you should also cross-reference this to the Professional Standards for QTS (see Appendix **page 129**) and start to complete the profiling required by your training provider.

Contents

Introduction

The information and activities in this section are aimed at practitioners who have increasing responsibility for teaching within the setting. This responsibility may include planning children's activities in an area of the setting, such as the role-play area, planning and teaching a group of children, or planning and teaching a story or lesson for the whole class. Some of you may have worked through all of the previous chapter, 'Making sense of the setting', and its activities. However, you may be starting your learning at this chapter, based on the evidence provided by completing the needs analysis exercise in Chapter 2, because of the experience you bring, perhaps from working as a teaching assistant or as a teacher in another phase. The activities described in this chapter can be carried out in any Foundation Stage setting, and across the areas of learning outlined in the *Curriculum Guidance*. Foundation Stage settings are complex places and this chapter is designed to support you as you begin to get to know, and make sense of, practice in the setting.

The *Curriculum Guidance for the Foundation Stage* identifies a number of principles which are '*drawn from, and are evident in, good and effective practice in early years settings*' (QCA, 2000, page 11). A summary of this book's coverage of the principles included in the *Curriculum Guidance* is given in an Appendix at the end of the book. It may be helpful to you to refer to this.

If you are training to be a teacher in the Foundation Stage you will need to audit your development by reference to the statements in *Qualifying to Teach Professional Standards for Qualified Teacher Status* (DfES/TTA, 2003), which sets out what a trainee teacher must know, understand and be able to do to be awarded QTS. A summary of the Standards that are addressed by different themes is also included as an Appendix. Please refer to this regularly.

As you complete each piece of evidence that accompanies the activities it is important that you share this with your supervising practitioner, school based mentor, colleagues and/or tutor, as relevant to your situation. This profiling process is particularly important for trainee teachers, and your training provider should advise you on this. Do ensure that you link the completion of the activities in this chapter with the profiling requirements of your training.

The matrix below outlines the content and activities for this chapter. Use it to help you plan your further learning. If you are a trainee teacher, use the summary of the Standards for the Award of Teacher Status to see how your experiences at this level can contribute directly to the profiling process.

	When finding out about policy and practice in the setting	When observing children	When observing other practitioners	When, evaluating planning or planning an activity or lesson	When teaching an activity or lesson	When reflecting on your practice
Young children as learners and enquirers		Observe children working at different activities and identify the types of learning approaches.	Observe the use of questioning by practitioners, and children's responses in a range of different activities.			Reflect on the ways in which you can provide opportunities for all learning approaches and adapt planning to do this. Reflect on the use of questioning to support learning.
Making connections in children's learning		Observe children in free and directed play. Record children conversing with one another and with you.		Plan for learning based on free play and directed play activities. Plan an activity to develop children's language.		Evaluate the differences in learning between the free play and directed play. Evaluate the ways in which children's language, vocabulary and thinking have been supported and how you might develop your verbal interactions with children.
Adults and children working together	Read the policy or handbook on partnership with parents. Analyse the type of information needed by members of the staff team and the strategies for sharing it.	Observe children's transitions from parent or carer to staff at the start of sessions.	Observe how practitioners exchange information within the setting.			Reflect on your observations and discuss these with colleagues. Reflect on how you could make more effective use of the strategies for sharing information between the team.
Organising the environment for learning		Observe children working as a whole group and in small groups.				Identify key issues associated with different group organisation, and evaluate the effectiveness of different forms of organisation.
Planning for learning	Become familiar with the medium term planning in the setting.			Plan an activity or lesson for a group or the whole class, based on assessment or observation of children's needs.	Ensure that your lesson plan contains all the required information.	Evaluate the children's learning and use this information to inform future teaching and learning activities. If possible, refine your planning and work with another group of children.
Observing and assessing young children	Become familiar with the areas of learning in the *Curriculum Guidance for the Foundation Stage*. Read the policy on assessment.	Use an observation schedule to systematically analyse children's development and learning in the areas of learning.	If possible, observe practitioners involving children in self-assessment.	Plan an activity that provides opportunities for children to assess their own learning. Plan ways in which you could model this to children.		Reflect on what you have learned about children's development and learning. Reflect on how you can support children's self-assessment and build this into your practice.

All the activities in this chapter are outlined in full and have the following information provided with them:

- essential background to the activity, including the use of resources and which context might be the most appropriate for carrying it out;
- suggested background reading;
- a description of the activity and all the elements that go to make it up;
- ideas on how to evaluate its success;
- your achievements.

Chapter 4   Young children as learners and enquirers

You have now had the opportunity to draw upon the work of Piaget, Vygotsky and Bruner and to identify theory in practice. You have also looked at particular features of how children learn and develop and this will be explored within this chapter and the final chapter of this theme. Other crucial features of how children learn: play, communication and schematic development will be addressed in the next theme in this chapter, 'Making connections in children's learning'. The need for children to feel safe and secure has already been discussed as a key feature in children's learning. It is now important to discuss more recent theory, which concentrates on the affective nature of how young children learn.

Emotional well-being

Laevers (1994) has drawn upon the theories of Piaget and Vygotsky to develop two ways of looking at how children are developing and learning. He states that children need to have high emotional well-being and high involvement in order to be learning. He devised a set of characteristics, which can be used to identify well-being and involvement as follows.

Well-being
- Openness.
- Flexibility.
- Self-confidence and self-esteem.
- Assertiveness.
- Vitality.
- Relaxation and inner peace.
- Enjoyment.
- The child feeling connected and in touch with him or herself.

Involvement
- Concentration.
- Energy.
- Complexity and creativity.
- Facial expression.
- Persistence.
- Precision.
- Reaction time.
- Language.
- Satisfaction.

When children are high on emotional well-being and involvement then they are motivated and confident to explore and to learn. The notion of emotional well-being and involvement being crucial to learning is also shown in the work of Goleman (1996) on emotional intelligence.

Emotional intelligence

Goleman (1996) emphasises how emotion is key to successful learning and that success in school is shaped by the emotional characteristics the child has developed prior to starting school. He lists the necessary characteristics which contribute to a child knowing how to learn. All are concerned with emotional intelligence:

- ○ confidence;
- ○ curiosity;
- ○ intentionality;
- ○ self-control;
- ○ relatedness;
- ○ capacity to communicate;
- ○ cooperativeness.

Children need to have high emotional well-being and intelligence in order to feel confident and take risks in their learning. This key factor for effective learning is also stated in the *Curriculum Guidance for the Foundation Stage* (QCA, 2000).

Example: *Yin is painting. She is engrossed in the activity putting paint onto the paintbrush and applying it to her paper. She then accidentally puts some paint on her fingers. She thoughtfully proceeds to carefully apply paint to her fingers and hands. When her hands are covered a teacher who has unobtrusively been watching her puts a clean sheet of paper on the table and indicates to Yin to place her hands on it. Yin smiles and laughs in wonder at the freshly made handprint.*

Learning in different ways and at different rates

QCA (2000) states that practitioners need to understand that children learn the same thing in different ways and that children learn at different rates. In order to be able to do this practitioners need, firstly, in-depth knowledge of child development and, secondly, to be able to link theoretical understanding of different ways children might learn to their practice.

Different ways of learning can be linked to Gardner's work on multiple intelligences. He identified eight learning capacities children develop as follows.

- ○ *Linguistic.* A capacity with language and patterns and a desire to explore them.
- ○ *Mathematical and logical.* A learner who succeeds at abstract, logical and structured thinking, discerning their relationships and underlying principles.
- ○ *Visual and spatial.* This intelligence relates to a facility with pictures and mental images, diagrams and graphical representation; the visual and spatial learner has a capacity to perceive the visual world accurately and will be able to transform and modify their perceptions.
- ○ *Musical.* Not only a capacity in composing and performing but also an ability to respond to mood and emotion, rhythm, timbre and structure in music.
- ○ *Interpersonal.* The capacity to establish good relationships with others, to discern mood, feelings and mental state in others and to communicate effectively.
- ○ *Intra-personal.* The capacity for self-awareness and self-knowledge and the ability to discern one's own emotions.
- ○ *Kinaesthetic.* The ability to use the body and objects in highly differentiated and skilled ways; the person with kinaesthetic intelligence likes to make and touch whilst learning.
- ○ *Naturalist.* The ability to recognise and categorise natural objects. (From Asprey *et al.*, 2002, page 12.)

Using these to identify a child's talents and abilities as well as looking at expected rates of development can enable practitioners to understand children and take them further in their learning.

Preparation
Arrange to observe a small number of children working at different activities. Look at the planning for the activities observed.

Task
Carry out observations of individual children and identify in which type of learning the child is engaged. Record the information using the following chart.

	Linguistic	Mathematical and logical	Visual and spatial	Musical	Interpersonal	Intra-personal	Kinaesthetic	Naturalist
Child 1								
Child 2								
Child 3								
Child 4								

Evaluation and follow up
Reflect on your observations using the following questions:

➲ Does each child use a range of learning approaches?
➲ Can you identify a pattern of learning for each child?
➲ Does the planning show opportunities for all learning approaches?
➲ Does the planning need to be adapted in the future to allow for children's different learning paths?

Attitudes and dispositions to learning

One of the principles enshrined in the *Curriculum Guidance for the Foundation Stage* (QCA, 2000) is that *'early years experience should build on what children already know and can do. It should also encourage a positive attitude and disposition to learn and aim to prevent early failure'* (page 11). Both Fisher (2002) and Katz (1998) identify developing positive dispositions to learning as being crucial if early learning is to be successful. Key dispositions are:

➲ motivation;
➲ determination;
➲ persistence;
➲ perseverance;
➲ curiosity.

The role of the adult is critical if children are to develop positive attitudes to learning. Again, this is outlined in QCA (2000), which states that effective teaching requires adults who can support and motivate children. Being positive with children can help them to develop positive attitudes to learning and the starting point should always be what the child can do. Refer back to Chapter 3 (**pages 43 to 45**) to refresh your memory about how adults in your setting encourage children to learn.

Questioning

QCA (2000) states that careful questioning is crucial for effective teaching. There are two main types of questions: firstly, closed questions, which require a yes or no answer and, secondly, open questions, which require children to think and expand on an answer. Using questions such as 'Can you …?' 'What if …?' 'How do you think …?' are all examples of open questions, which require children to actively engage with what is being asked of them. Siraj-Blatchford *et al.* (2002) list open-ended questioning as one of the requirements for positive outcomes in children's learning. Dowling (1992, Chapter 6) gives useful hints on how to be an effective questioner. For example, giving children time to respond, and not asking questions to which you obviously know the answer.

Preparation

Plan to observe a whole group time, small group time and independent activity time. Focus on the teacher's questioning style during each observation.

Task

Carry out your observations. Use the following grid to analyse your findings.

Type of activity	Question by practitioner	Response by child	Analysis
Whole group time			
Small group time			
Independent activity			

Evaluation and follow up

Evaluate your observations using the following questions:

➲ What was the frequency of open and closed questions?
➲ Were different types of questions used during the different activities?
➲ How did the children respond to the different types of questions?
➲ What language did the children use when responding to the different types of questions?
➲ What learning were the children engaged in when responding to the different types of questions?

Your achievements

Now you have read this section and completed the activities you should be able to:

➲ understand the importance of emotional well-being for children's learning;
➲ understand that high well-being results in confident children who are willing and able to take risks in their learning;
➲ identify different learning paths that children can and do use;
➲ reflect upon your planning and how it caters for children's developmental and learning needs;
➲ understand what is meant by and identify positive attitudes and dispositions to learning in children;
➲ begin to understand how to promote positive dispositions through example;
➲ understand the different types of questions that can be used in teaching and their effect upon children's learning.

If you feel that you have completed the tasks successfully, return to the relevant needs analysis and mark it off with the date and evidence. If appropriate, ask your tutor about being able to use this as evidence of your understanding or professional capability. This information could be used as part of the course you are studying. This may be evidence towards the Professional Standards for QTS or it might be part of a profile or an assignment you might be completing as part of your studies. Please refer to the tables at the back of the book (**page 129**), which detail coverage against the principles listed within the *Curriculum Guidance for the Foundation Stage* as well as the Professional Standards for QTS.

Chapter 4 · Making connections in children's learning

In Chapters 2 and 3 you have had the opportunity to consider the process of play and to identify quality play. In this chapter you need to engage with your role as a practitioner in providing for play. However, first of all it is important to gain some understanding of the debate about structured and unstructured play and free and directed play.

Structured and unstructured play

Manning and Sharp's (1977) research on provision for children's play focused on the notion of structured play provision for young children. By their definition, unstructured play was then seen as any play not provided by the practitioner. This suggested that structured play was preferable to unstructured play. However, as Moyles (1989) shows, play is always structured. Children's play is structured by the materials and resources that they play with, and by the ideas that the children bring to the play situation. Therefore, quality play is dependent upon the practitioner providing a challenging environment for play.

Free play and directed play

Free play is the opportunity to explore resources and to play without adult-imposed outcomes. Directed play is play that has an adult-imposed outcome. Moyles (1989) sees these two types of play as having different and unique learning outcomes. Free play allows for exploration and directed play allows mastery, both of which are necessary for children. Both of these ways of playing are supported by QCA (2000) when discussing the role of the practitioner in play:

'The role of the practitioner is crucial in:

➲ *supporting children's learning through planned play activity;*
➲ *extending and supporting children's spontaneous play'* (page 25).

Preparation
Plan a play activity for a small group of children. In your planning you should allow children time to explore and make sense of your chosen resources – free play. You also need to plan for children to gain mastery of your chosen resources and achieve the learning objectives.

Show your plans to your practitioner and discuss your ideas. Amend your plans, if necessary, following your discussion.

Task

According to your plans, work with a small group of children giving them time for free play and directed play. Observe them at play and make notes of your observations. Use the following table to analyse your findings.

	Free play – areas of learning	Directed play – areas of learning
Child 1		
Child 2		
Child 3		
Child 4		
Child 5		
Child 6		

Evaluation and follow up

Reflect on and evaluate your observations using the following questions.

➲ How did the children play in the free play situation?
➲ How did the children play in the directed play situation?
➲ Discuss whether or not all the children achieved the learning objectives? Which areas of learning were addressed in the free play situation?
➲ Which areas of learning were addressed in the directed play situation?
➲ What were the differences in learning between the two play situations?
➲ Discuss your findings with your practitioner.

Creativity and cross-curricular links

In the previous chapters the creative process has been outlined and you should now have an understanding of the stages children go through during the creative process. Now you need to consider how creativity can foster the development of the whole child through looking at creativity and cross-curricular links. Duffy in Siraj-Blatchford (1998) supports this by stating, *'creativity is a part of every subject area'* (page 144). This can be developed through the six areas of learning in the following ways.

Creativity and social, emotional and personal development

By engaging in the creative process children will be developing many of the dispositions and attitudes necessary for healthy personal, social and emotional development. Being curious means that children are alert and interested and they are motivated to learn. Whilst in this phase of the creative process they are also attentive and involved.

Creativity and communication, language and literacy

Making up their own stories, songs, rhymes and poems is one of the early learning goals (QCA, 2000, page 50). Creating stories enables children to engage with the final aspect of the creative process.

Example: *Using the story of* Goldilocks and the Three Bears *as a stimulus, George, a three year old in the nursery said, 'My story is called Sophie and the three cats. There is a mummy, daddy and a baby and Sophie takes them on holiday'.*

Creativity and mathematical development

Craft (2000) discusses a mathematical approach, which involves conjecture and possibility. The use of 'what if' language, which allows children to play with mathematical possibilities involves them in the creative process.

Example: *Amber is playing in the small world area. She is placing beds in different rooms of the house. As she plays she talks to Cameron 'What if we put a bed in this room then we will need four people in the house'.*

Creativity and knowledge and understanding of the world

'Asking questions about why things happen and how things work' (QCA, 2000, page 88) is an early learning goal for exploration and investigation. Asking questions about the world around them engages children at all levels of the creative process.

Creativity and physical development

Working towards many of the early learning goals for physical development can involve children in the creative process. Outdoor play where children can build and use assault courses made out of blocks, planks, tyres and other assorted equipment will enable children to be controlled and co-ordinated, to travel in different ways, to gain an awareness of space and to use equipment as well as be creative.

Creative development

All aspects of creative development should engage children in creativity. Painting a picture, making a model or inventing a dance should enable children to engage in all levels of the creative process. However, Duffy (2003) makes the important distinction between representation and reproduction. Representing a flower through a range of creative media using their own style is being creative. Reproducing a yellow daffodil using materials presented and prepared by the adult and in the style of the adult is not creative.

Language and communication

In the previous chapter you identified and observed how children's language develops. In this chapter you need to gain an understanding of how you can interact with children to support and extend their developing language. QCA (2000) explicitly states that effective teaching requires *using language that is rich and using correct grammar. Recognising that what is said and how the practitioner speaks is the main way of teaching new vocabulary and helping children to develop linguistic structures'* (page 23). Adults do this through:

- ⊃ listening to children;
- ⊃ being sensitive to what children say and what children mean;
- ⊃ modelling language;
- ⊃ extending language;
- ⊃ having informal conversations with children;
- ⊃ asking questions (discussed on **pages 71 to 72**);
- ⊃ giving children opportunities to initiate language as well as respond.

It is important to note that modelling correct language is a more effective and acceptable way of helping to develop children's language than correcting their language, which can be negative.

Preparation

Prepare to work with a small group of children. Plan an activity that involves children in talking and conversing with one another and with you, and prepare to tape record the small group session.

Task

Carry out your planned activity with the children and tape record the session. Transcribe the recorded session and analyse your interactions with the children.

Evaluation and follow up

Reflect on and evaluate your observations using the following questions:

- How have you developed the children's vocabulary?
- How have you developed the children's language?
- How have you developed the children's thinking?
- Is there evidence of children's language and thinking not being developed?
- Was there an over-emphasis on some types of communication strategies? For example, questioning.
- Did you modify your language in response to different children?
- How did you engage less talkative children?
- Was time given for children to talk with one another?
- Were opportunities given for children to initiate interactions as well as respond?
- How could you develop your verbal interactions with children?

Your achievements

Now you have read this section and completed the activities you should be able to:

- understand the difference between structured and unstructured play;
- understand the difference between free play and directed play;
- identify the creative process across all learning areas;
- understand and evaluate your own role in developing children's language.

If you feel that you have completed the tasks successfully, return to the relevant needs analysis and mark it off with the date and evidence. If appropriate, ask your tutor about being able to use this as evidence of your understanding or professional capability. This information could be used as part of the course you are studying. This may be evidence towards the Professional Standards for QTS or it might be part of a profile or an assignment you might be completing as part of your studies. Please refer to the tables at the back of the book which detail coverage against the principles listed within the *Curriculum Guidance for the Foundation Stage* as well as the Professional Standards for QTS.

Adults and children working together

In Chapter 2 you will have explored the reasons why the partnership with parents as co-educators is recognised as a principle of practice in the Foundation Stage. In this section you will observe how the staff team relate to and work with parents. You will also learn more about the work of the team on a day-to-day basis. You will develop a deeper understanding of the ways in which information is exchanged formally and informally within the staff team and with parents.

Understanding current policies and practices within the setting

Most settings will have either:

➲ a policy which sets out the principles which guide the partnership with parents; or
➲ a handbook which gives information about this relationship.

Many settings will have both. It is important to obtain copies of these documents as they will set out the way that the staff in the setting value parental involvement, and the strategies they adopt to further this.

> 'The good Foundation Stage teacher ... knows that if parents and carers feel welcome and valued, the children are more likely to feel the same ... We must remember that parents, too, come with different experiences, and by making space for them to come into the nursery with their children, and providing displays explaining what the children might be doing and why, we can involve parents in their children's learning. This could influence the ways in which they will support their children later in their school lives.' (Moyles, 2002, page 21)

Fisher (2002) suggests a range of strategies for developing parental partnership, including visits, special events, two-way communication of information and expression of hopes and values.

> 'Conversations with parents can benefit all parties concerned. It benefits teachers because of their increased knowledge of the child, it benefits parents by making them genuine partners in their child's learning and it benefits children, who see home and school as mutually interested in their education.' (Fisher, 2002, page 25)

In Chapter 2 you learned the importance of the day-to-day informal contacts with parents and have considered the need to be aware of child safety issues. These are the occasions when much valuable interaction and exchange of information takes place. You are now going to observe this interaction more closely, to understand the way that staff in the setting and parents engage in this important two-way flow of information and maintain this key relationship. Edgington (1998, page 72) stresses that staff must organise their time so that they are on hand and are welcoming at the beginning and end of a session to talk to parents and carers. This is particularly important for those who are least confident in the school situation.

Preparation

Read copies of the policy for parental partnership and/or the information provided for parents.

Task

For two or three days, whilst the children are arriving or leaving the setting, observe how your colleagues relate to the parents. It might be helpful for you to involve yourself with the children so that you can observe unobtrusively. Try to observe the way the transition from home to school takes place. Once the parents have left and the session has begun, make brief notes on your observations.

Evaluation and follow up

At the end of this period, reflect on your observations. Ask yourself the following questions:

- How did the transition from parent to staff take place? Was it different from one parent to another?
- Was any news given of important family events? How did the staff respond? Was the child involved?
- Was any important information about the child passed from parent to staff, or staff to parent?
- Did I observe anxiety in any parent? How was their anxiety dealt with?
- Did I observe anxiety in any child? How was their anxiety dealt with?

Discuss your observations with the staff involved. What was their perception of the interactions you observed?

Getting to know families better

The staff in the setting will be keen to invite parents to events and special occasions. Typically these might include:

- singalongs;
- parties;
- picnics;
- class assemblies;
- curriculum workshops;
- open days.

Activities such as these help to build trust and greater understanding, and it is often during informal exchanges that staff can gain insights into individual children's backgrounds, which may prove valuable in their relationships with the children. It is very important that you, together with other staff members, recognise that children belong to families and communities and that they do not exist in isolation. When they arrive in nursery or school they have already learned a huge amount, acquired many attitudes and skills and assimilated much of their cultural heritage. These factors, together with the individual child's personality will profoundly affect his or her social orientation and ability and disposition to learn.

Families getting to know the staff and one another

The activities and occasions mentioned above also present opportunities for parents and carers to become more familiar with the staff and to realise that their contribution to the process is valued and that ' *the past and future part played by parents in the education of their children is recognised and explicitly encouraged*' (QCA, 2000, page 9). In our multicultural society, social events within the school or nursery also give families opportunities to get to know one another, to share ideas, common concerns, food and different aspects of their cultures, helping to overcome prejudice and to promote good, non-judgemental attitudes and better community relations.

Information for families about the setting and wider issues

There will usually be a notice board near the entrance. This will give information about the current topic and activities and ideas for parents and carers to develop some aspects of the work with their children. This information may sometimes also be provided in community languages. This may include information about:

⊃ forthcoming events such as outings, picnics, special visitors to the setting;
⊃ projects requiring volunteers for activities such as helping to maintain equipment, working in the garden, looking after a pet during a holiday period;
⊃ names, addresses and contact numbers for various agencies such as Women's Aid, the Council for Racial Equality, local clinics and health centres, library, community centre, play group, mother and toddler group and Sure Start centre.

Settling children into the setting

Settings adopt a variety of strategies for settling children into their new situation and routines. In some cases entry is staggered with children admitted in small groups over a period of time. Sometimes all of the children are admitted for a short period each day, and the length of the session is then gradually increased.

Parents are usually encouraged to stay for a short time to ensure the child is settled. Some parents may not recognise the need for this support, and will need an explanation. In some instances this support will need to continue over a longer period, depending on the individual child and this would be negotiated between staff and parents. In some cases it is the parent rather than the child who is anxious about the separation, and this, too, needs sensitive handling.

Providing services for families

In addition to this regular informal contact, many settings have more formal systems for exchanging information and provide other services for families. This could include:

⊃ home school diaries, where important information is recorded by staff and parents or carers;
⊃ reading and mathematics records that are sent home daily or weekly;
⊃ formal parent consultation meetings, usually once or twice each year.

Schools also support families by sharing resources. Children and parents together may choose toys or books to use at home.

Other professionals who provide services

A number of other professionals contribute to the work of the setting. The most frequent visitors are likely to be those who have a responsibility for the well-being or health of young children and their families. These will include the following.

Health visitor
Health visitors look after the health and well-being of children from a few days following birth until statutory school age. They are usually attached to local surgeries or health centres and work in close collaboration with family doctors. In many nurseries they visit regularly and provide a valuable link between family and staff and also through contacts with other agencies, some of whom are detailed below.

School nurse
Employed by the local health authority, school nurses takes over responsibility for children when they enter the Reception class. They provide information, health and parenting advice. Nurses liaise between the school and the local area health authority if there are serious health issues under consideration. They will obtain and pass on information about notifiable diseases such as measles, scarlet fever or tuberculosis.

A range of other people with professional or community interests may also visit the setting. This is discussed in more detail in Chapter 5, **page 107**.

Children's Centres

Plans have been announced by the Department for Education and Skills for Children's Centres modelled on successful integrated family centres, where a range of health, social and educational services are integrated to provide a holistic approach to the care and education of the children. These will now be managed, organised and run under the Sure Start Unit. For further information on this refer to the Sure Start website at www.surestart.org.uk.

Working as a team

It is important that members of the staff team communicate and share ideas and information on a number of levels. At one level, a shared philosophy of the Foundation Stage is needed, which in turn informs the provision in the setting. Developing a shared philosophy is discussed in more detail in Chapter 5 on **page 106**. On a day-to-day basis, team members also need to have systems for exchanging information of a practical nature, relating to the needs of individual children or to the setting as a whole. In reality, this can be difficult in a busy early years setting, particularly if some staff are in the setting for limited periods of time. For example, the bi-lingual assistant may work in a number of classes, and as a consequence may only work in the nursery for about an hour of each session.

Staff will exchange information on an ongoing, informal basis throughout the day. In addition there will be planned opportunities for this. Strategies will vary but are likely to include regular meetings before and after each session, weekly planning meetings, shared setting diary and notice board, entries in child profiles and shared lesson plans. There will also be regular team meetings with an agreed agenda. Members of the team will bring different perceptions, levels of experience and expertise to this exchange, and these should be valued and respected. Utilising the experience and interests of all the members of the team will enrich the provision for the children and life in the setting. For example, bi-lingual assistants may have in-depth knowledge of the cultural inheritance of particular children in the setting.

Preparation
Make a list of the systems in use in your setting for exchanging information on a day-to-day basis.

Task
Using a pro forma such as that shown below, record and analyse the type of information needed on a day-to-day basis and the ways in which information is shared.

Strategy	Purpose	Type of information shared
Weekly meeting of the team		
Setting diary		
Notice board		
Informal meeting prior to session start		
Child profiles		
Planning meetings		
Lesson or activity plans		
Other		

Evaluation and follow up
Which of these strategies have you been involved in? Are there any you could be using more effectively? Discuss this with your mentor.

Your achievements

Now that you have read this section and completed the activities you should be able to:

⊃ understand the current policies and practices within the setting in which you are working;
⊃ recognise the strategies which can be used to support relationships between home and setting;
⊃ consider the different roles and responsibilities of a range of professionals who work in partnership with the setting;
⊃ explore and evaluate the systems in place to exchange information between team members;
⊃ review the procedures in place to ensure good communication systems between all team members;
⊃ contribute to the effective working of the team.

If you feel that you have completed the tasks successfully, return to the relevant needs analysis and mark it off with the date and evidence. If appropriate, ask your tutor about being able to use this as evidence of your understanding or professional capability. This information could be used as part of the course you are studying. This may be evidence towards the Professional Standards for QTS or it might be part of a profile or an assignment you might be completing as part of your studies. Please refer to the tables at the back of the book which detail coverage against the principles listed within the *Curriculum Guidance for the Foundation Stage* as well as the Professional Standards for QTS.

Organising the learning environment

The active nature of children's learning requires an environment that provides *'well-planned, purposeful play'* with learning opportunities *'that have been planned by adults and those that are initiated by children'* (QCA, 2000, page 11). In this chapter we look at play and child initiated activity, and the organisation of the environment to support whole group and small group adult initiated activity.

Managing an environment where play is integral to learning

By now you will realise that being responsible for an early years setting involves complex and challenging organisation and management. While carrying out the tasks linked to the previous sections the children will have been playing. There is an ideological belief that children make no distinction between work and play. However, this is questionable. In practice many children talk about play and work and see them as different because teachers differentiate between work and play. This need not be the case if practitioners believe in planning and organising an interactive environment where the responsibility for learning is shared between adults and children and where play is seen as *'a key way in which young children learn with enjoyment and challenge'* (QCA, 2000, page 25).

Managing whole group and small group teaching

Efficient deployment of time for both children and adults is important. As a part of all aspects of children's learning there is a need to work in small and large groups. The organisation of these groups will depend on adult pedagogy and a range of pressures already discussed. The way in which groups are organised and the rationale behind what teaching and learning takes place in groups is key to their effectiveness (Fisher, 2002a).

You will find that teaching the *whole class* may be expedient at times. It should be approached, however, with a health warning! Pollard (1997, page 210) discusses class work as being useful *'for stimulating children's thinking, exploring ideas (and) asking more probing questions ...'*. He goes on to consider the strain put on teachers and children when there is insufficient time for consultation with individuals and difficulty in matching the task to children's needs. There are additional problems with whole class teaching for very young children.

Effective teaching of *small groups* will only be possible if the organisation for teaching and learning is based on independence, trust and skilled organisation and planning. Fisher (2002a) says that learning is most successful when teachers facilitate and support children's learning in response to what children need to initiate. Teachers have a responsibility to introduce children to skills, knowledge and understanding but should ensure that children have ownership of experiences and understand the relevance they have to their own lives. How do these ideas relate to children working as a whole group, in small groups or to those working individually?

Preparation
Identify the times of day when each type of activity takes place and negotiate with other members of staff the best time to observe. Make your observations over a two-week period.

Task

Carry out some informal observations of whole group organisation and keep a record of:

➲ how many times and how long children spend in a whole group situation;
➲ where whole group sessions take place;
➲ the content of the group session.

Continue your observations with small groups and with children working individually. Consider:

➲ what types of activities are children initiating themselves;
➲ what evidence is there of children's motivation, exploration and positive disposition for learning;
➲ what examples have you found of creative and imaginative work;
➲ what do you feel about the quality of the tasks that have been set for the children?

Consider the ways in which children are organised. Are they:

➲ self-selected with children working on child initiated, co-operative activities;
➲ selected by the teacher according to a number of criteria and working on a teacher-initiated activities;
➲ working alongside other children but concentrating on individual tasks?

Evaluation and follow up

From your observations what are your conclusions about children working in small groups or as a whole group? A typical response to the exercise might be that children are spending too long sitting in an uncomfortable position, on a carpet, unable to see. They may be receiving undifferentiated information with requests for answers that are outside their experience. There may be no recognition of their prior understanding and little chance for them to communicate effectively or to work creatively or independently.

What are the key issues that have resulted from your observations?

What positive information/concerns have you noted?

At this point you have had experience of working in and observing and evaluating aspects of the learning environment. You are ready to use the evidence from your observations with the Foundation Stage team to reflect on current practice and negotiate for change.

Your achievements

Now you have read this section and completed the activities you should be able to:

➲ recognise that there can be a tension between play and work;
➲ evaluate the use of physical space;
➲ evaluate activities and their relevance for the needs of the children;
➲ observe a group of children working or playing and reflect on the possible changes to encourage a more creative and independent approach to learning.

If you feel that you have completed the tasks successfully, return to the relevant needs analysis and mark it off with the date and evidence. If appropriate, ask your tutor about being able to use this as evidence of your understanding or professional capability. This information could be used as part of the course you are studying. This may be evidence towards the Professional Standards for QTS or it might be part of a profile or an assignment you might be completing as part of your studies. Please refer to the tables at the back of the book which detail coverage against the principles listed within the *Curriculum Guidance for the Foundation Stage* as well as the Professional Standards for QTS.

In your practice to date you have become acquainted with the planning in place within your setting and looked at this planning in the light of the areas of learning in the Foundation Stage guidance. You have also become aware of the differing theoretical or pedagogical approaches to the education of young children that underpin or inform the curriculum provision in the Foundation Stage. You will now begin to plan a range of teaching activities for small groups of children, or for an area of the setting or classroom.

In this section you will begin to address additional aspects of curriculum provision such as how children's experience and learning to date should inform planning. This is a vital aspect of planning, and is recognised as a central principle of effective planning in the Foundation Stage. It is the way in which the practitioner can be confident that planned activities respond to the needs of the child. Specifically, you will learn about:

➲ the observation/assessment and planning cycle;
➲ differentiation;
➲ adult and child initiated planning;
➲ evaluating learning;
➲ lesson planning.

Starting from the child

The notion of child-centredness, memorably expressed by Fisher (2002) in the title of her book, is the overriding principle that should always guide planning and teaching. This is a cyclical process:

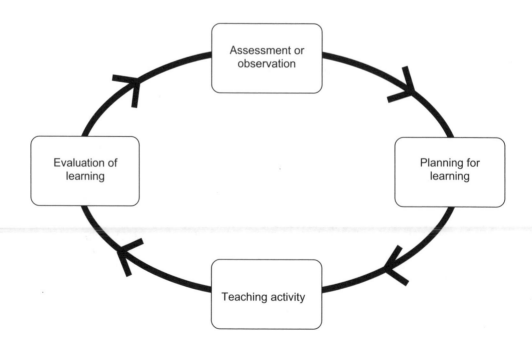

Fisher (2002, page 45) regards this as one of the principles of early childhood education. She states: '*Our starting points for supporting learning are what children can do and what they can nearly do, so that children should be helped to identify their own targets and achievements and observation-based assessment should be the basis for planning.*'

This view is echoed throughout the literature on early childhood education and is confirmed by research (Pascal and Bertram, 1997; Whalley, 2001; Webber, 1999; Fisher, 2002; Whitebread, 2003). It is also a principle of the *Curriculum Guidance for the Foundation Stage*, which states that: *'to be effective, an early years curriculum should be carefully structured …[including] provision for the starting points from which children develop their learning, building on what they can already do …'* (QCA, 2000, page 11).

Differentiation

If the planning is to be based on the needs of the child, as determined by observation or assessment of what the child can do, then it is clear that the planned activity will need to be designed so that children, either singly or in a group, are likely to be successful when they undertake it. This process is called differentiation: making subtle changes to a planned activity so that children of different attainment are able to learn from it. When you are planning lessons or activities you must consider how the task can be differentiated so that all of the children can achieve success, and this can be approached in a number of ways.

You may plan different tasks for children so that the activity they undertake is well matched to their current understanding. There are alternative ways of differentiating which do not involve giving children different tasks. For example, when working with a group of children you can ask more or less challenging questions, depending on the child's level of understanding or development. When considering how to differentiate questions, it is important to bear in mind the child's language development, which is discussed in more detail in Chapter 3, **page 48**. Whatever differentiation strategy you adopt, it must be thought through when you are planning the lesson or activity.

Whitebread (2003) suggests that four specific approaches to differentiation are appropriate to children in the early years:

➲ Outcome: children undertake the same task or activity; the outcome differs according to the child's ability or developmental stage.
➲ Support: different levels of adult support are provided according to the child's needs.
➲ Recording method: all of the children have the same task, but the way that their thinking, findings or understanding is recorded differs. For example, some may write, some draw and some describe their findings in a science activity.
➲ Complexity: all of the children attempt tasks that are based on a shared theme or activity; the tasks are of varying difficulty, according to their developmental level.

Differentiation should be a consideration during every planned activity, based on the ability, interest or developmental level of the children. As you plan your lessons you should consider and record how you intend to differentiate the activity.

Adult and child initiated planning

Another of the principles for early years education outlined in the Foundation Stage guidance (QCA, 2000, page 11) is that there should be opportunities for children to engage in activities that they initiate for themselves. There are a number of ways in which you can approach this principle.

Capturing the moment

By maintaining an ethos which is responsive to children's ideas, experiences and achievements you can ensure that their contribution to planning is encouraged. Sometimes a child will arrive with news, artefacts or 'work' that needs an immediate response. It is always important to make time to value this aspect of children's lives.

Example: *Mia comes into school with news that her cat has had kittens. The children talk excitedly about pets and baby animals. The practitioner draws their attention to the classroom books about animals and collects some additional books from the school library for them to look at. Some children decide to make a record of the different pets that children in the class own, and they are encouraged to record this as a simple data handling exercise.*

A responsive ethos
Sometimes the children come up with their own ideas or initiatives that provide attractive starting points for a series of activities. They may respond to a planned activity, or play with toys or equipment in a way that prompts you to rethink or modify your future planning.

Example: *Large building blocks are part of the equipment in the nursery. A group of children have used them to build a large 'boat', which they love playing in. The nursery staff adapt their planning in communication, language and literacy to include some new stories and poems that involve boats. The children are delighted with these new stories. Later, the staff provide some materials with which the children can make boats that they can float in the water tray.*

In order to allow children's experience to inform your practice in this way it is vital to allow time to observe children working and playing. In particular, you need to take account of the ways that they use the tools and materials they are given. In this way you are better able to change and develop teaching approaches in response to children's needs and to adapt your planning accordingly. The importance of observation as an assessment strategy and as an ongoing source of information for the practitioner is discussed in Chapter 3 **page 60**.

Eliciting children's ideas and experience
It is important when planning a new activity or sequence of activities that you elicit children's interests and current level of understanding. Planning will be enriched by talking to children about their own experience before planning an aspect of the curriculum in detail.

Example: *The staff in the Reception classes meet regularly to plan together. Before planning a topic on 'celebrations' they talk to the children in their classes about celebrations they have taken part in. As a result of this discussion with the children they plan their activities around the children's experiences of birth and wedding rites from several faith communities and cultures.*

Allowing for the unexpected
Perhaps this should really be regarded as planning for the unplannable! As a Foundation Stage practitioner you should recognise that planning must be flexible and responsive to events that may occur in the children's lives at home and in school. Sometimes, an unexpected event may provide opportunities that are too good to miss for enriching children's experience.

Example: *The gardener turns up unexpectedly to cut the grass on the football field adjoining the nursery garden. From behind the safety of the fence the children watch her driving the large grass mower. The nursery staff encourage them to watch closely; the children are fascinated by the noise made by the mower, the huge wheels and the rotating cutters. They talk about the grass cutting. Gregor knows that cut grass is used to feed horses and ponies in the winter. Jessica says that if her dog eats grass it means that 'he has a bad tummy' but that her rabbit eats grass all the time. Nazir talks about the grass being cut at his dad's cricket club. Later, when the gardener has finished they go and collect some cut grass, although the staff are careful not to expose children with allergies to the cut grass. They smell it and examine the way that the sap stains tissue paper. They discuss how most plants are green and the teacher explains the science of chlorophyll in very simple terms.*

Example: *Overnight, a storm has blown lots of autumn leaves into the Reception class doorway. The children go out and play with the leaves, scuffing through them and scrunching them up with their hands. Encouraged by the staff they bring some leaves into the classroom and write a class poem about the colours and texture of the leaves.*

Sometimes it is children's interpretations of a situation, the meaning they bring to it or their misunderstandings that may prompt you to make changes to your planning, or to plan new activities. You may be able to respond immediately to correct misunderstandings; alternatively, you may have to change your planning or include some new activities.

Example: *In reception, Jake has brought in a 'map' he has drawn, which he shows to the class. He tells the children it is a map of England and points out various places. Bethan, whose parents were born in Cardiff, asks 'What about Wales?' Rebecca follows this up by asking 'What about dolphins?'*

The practitioner can follow up on these misunderstandings immediately, and may decide to include in future planned activities some work using simple maps.

As well as responding to children's current understanding when planning, it is important to include child initiated topics when planning.

Evaluating learning and teaching

It is important for your developing professional practice that you reflect on and evaluate children's learning and your own teaching. Make brief notes about the activity or lesson, focusing on whether the children met, exceeded or failed to meet the learning objective. If the lesson or activity did not go as well as you hoped, think about what you might do differently in future. In the Foundation Stage much teaching and learning is planned for small groups so you have the opportunity to repeat an activity with several groups. This means that you have additional opportunities to reflect on and refine your planning. When planning lessons or activities you may have slightly different versions of the plan to differentiate the activity for a particular group. When you teach the same lesson or activity several times you also have the opportunity to refine the plan before teaching another group. This is particularly useful if it becomes clear after your first experience that you have seriously misjudged the activity or the needs of the children!

When you evaluate, do not write long descriptions of the lesson or activity. Instead, reflect on the experience, note whether the children met the learning objectives and make brief comments about your own professional practice.

You will need to devise a format for recording all of this information, and an example is given below. The setting may have its own format for recording this information.

Children who surpassed the learning objectives

Name	Extension work required

Children who did not achieve the learning objectives

Name	Area of concern

Preparation

For this task you will plan an activity for a group of children. Depending on your setting, this might be a story, an activity or lesson for a group or for the whole class. It could also be an informal activity, which children can choose to take part in if they wish to.

Look at the weekly or medium-term planning for your class or setting. Choose an aspect of the planning for your focus. This may be a lesson that is to be taught to the whole group, or to small groups. It could also be an activity which children may take part in if they choose to.

You may need to elicit children's understanding of the topic, or facilitate their expression of their own ideas, so that these can be fed into your planning. Explore the topic in discussion with them. If you are planning an activity for an area of the classroom or setting it might inform your planning if you take time to observe how children currently use the tools, materials or equipment in that area. This may suggest the approach you should adopt, or a starting point.

Devising a lesson or activity plan
A plan for a lesson or activity will need to cover the following areas:

- ⇒ date and time of the lesson or activity;
- ⇒ title or general description including the area of learning;
- ⇒ previous observation or assessment information;
- ⇒ specific learning objectives;
- ⇒ vocabulary and key questions;
- ⇒ resources;
- ⇒ organisation, including the use of ICT where appropriate;
- ⇒ differentiation;
- ⇒ evaluation of children's learning.

Previous observation or assessment information
The importance of matching the lesson or activity to children's needs has already been explored. This means that your observation or assessment of children's current level of understanding or development should be the starting point for your lesson plan.

Objectives for children's learning

Learning objectives for the children (sometimes referred to as learning outcomes) must be clear and specific, based on the knowledge, skills or understanding which is the focus of the lesson. They may include aspects of children's social and personal development as well as cognitive or skills objectives.

The following is the first part of one of the Early Learning Goals of the Curriculum Guidance for the Foundation Stage:

'Recognise and explore how sounds can be changed …'

Although this is only part of one of the Early Learning Goals, it is still too complex a learning objective for one lesson or activity. The objective for a lesson or activity might better be expressed as:

When playing the instruments, the children will recognise the difference between fast and slow.

Learning objectives should express exactly that, what the children will learn. They are not simply a statement of the task undertaken.

The following is not a useful objective as it does not tell you what the children will learn:

'The children will sort the shapes.' This would be better expressed as:

'The children will recognise the difference between circles and squares.'

Key questions and vocabulary

Think about the key questions you will need to ask to support and develop children's understanding. What vocabulary will you need to revise or introduce? If you have thought this through in advance you are much less likely to use vocabulary or forms of expression that the children do not understand. Important vocabulary and key questions should be recorded on your lesson plan.

Resources

What resources will you need for the lesson or activity? Do you need to reserve shared equipment (such as audio visual, science, technology or music resources) or borrow them from another class? Do you need to make any resources?

Organisation and structure of the lesson or activity

Think about the content, timing and sequence of the lesson or activity. If this is a whole class lesson, consider how the children will be grouped and how you and any other adults in the class will be employed.

The structure will include the introduction and main teaching input, follow-up activities, and summary or plenary to consolidate learning at the end of the lesson. Think about how you will introduce the lesson.

- ⮞ How will you capture the children's attention and interest at the beginning?
- ⮞ How will you make the learning objective clear to them?
- ⮞ What are the key points you want to communicate?

You will need to make some notes in your lesson plan of the main points you hope to address and it may be a good idea to go over these as you plan. Try to avoid writing a lengthy 'script' of what you plan to say as this can lead to a rather wooden delivery when you are with the children.

What will be the follow up activities for the children? You will need to consider the implications for organisation when planning these.

How will you bring the activity or lesson to an end and revise the main points? Will the children be able to show or present the results of their work to others, if appropriate?

When planning the activities the children will complete, it is important that the task will motivate them and engage their interest. Avoid worksheets and other low-level tasks: children learn better by actively engaging with their learning. It is often difficult to estimate how long it will take for children to complete a task. Something you have spent a long time planning for and preparing may be finished in a few minutes, so it is always a good idea to plan a follow up activity for early finishers or to challenge children further. If the activity is too difficult or too formal for the children they may become frustrated, bored and demotivated.

Differentiation

Are there different learning objectives, activities, or teaching strategies to meet the needs of children, especially if this is a whole class lesson? How will other adults be involved in supporting differentiation?

Evaluation of children's learning

At the end of the lesson or activity you will need to make some evaluation of whether the children have met the learning outcome. This may be done by discussion, observation or assessment of the work they have produced. Whatever method you use, it is important for your future planning to identify those children who have not met the learning objectives and those who have exceeded them.

Teach the lesson or activity. Make sure that all of the resources are prepared before you start the session.

Evaluation and follow up

Review the lesson or activity. What went well? What did the children learn? Did all the children meet the learning objectives? If not, what could you do differently? How were your initial thoughts developed by responding to your observations, elicitation of children's current understanding or your exploration of their ideas?

If it is possible, and after you have evaluated the session, adapt your plan and work with another group of children. Re-evaluate the learning. Was the activity sufficiently differentiated to meet the needs of all of the children in the group?

Your achievements

Now that you have read this section and completed the activities you should be able to:

➲ understand that planning is based on the needs of the child;
➲ recognise the cyclical nature of the observation or assessment, planning, teaching and evaluation process;
➲ understand the process of differentiation, and differentiate activities to meet children's needs;
➲ recognise the need to include child-initiated activities in your planning;
➲ plan and teach lessons or sequences of lessons drawn from the medium term planning;
➲ evaluate the children's learning and amend your planning based on this information;
➲ refine and develop your planning to reflect child-initiated activities.

If you feel that you have completed the tasks successfully, return to the relevant needs analysis and mark it off with the date and evidence. If appropriate, ask your tutor about being able to use this as evidence of your understanding or professional capability. This information could be used as part of the course you are studying. This may be evidence towards the Professional Standards for QTS or it might be part of a profile or an assignment you might be completing as part of your studies. Please refer to the tables at the back of the book which detail coverage against the principles listed within the *Curriculum Guidance for the Foundation Stage* as well as the Professional Standards for QTS.

Observing and assessing young children

The focus of your work at this level will be on extending and refining the range of observation techniques that you use as well as considering how to respond to this information. You have previously explored and practised how to observe and listen to children as well as how to begin interpreting some of the evidence that you gathered through those observations.

It is essential that you decide which children to assess as well as how and when to assess children's development and learning as an integral part of the planning process. This will ensure that you are using a range of observation strategies to gather all the different kinds of evidence, which you will need to inform your teaching. It also ensures that as part of a Foundation Stage team, all the adults within the setting are clear about what they need to be doing in terms of their roles and responsibilities in relation to assessment and record keeping.

Consider how other adults working in the setting/classroom can be involved in this assessment process. It might be helpful to ask yourself the following questions adapted from Fisher (2002, page 190).

Who will gather the evidence, where and when?
Who? (adults)
➲ the practitioner;
➲ another adult (such as a nursery nurse or teaching assistant).

With whom? (the children)
➲ child alone;
➲ children together;
➲ children working with the practitioner;
➲ children working with another adult.

Where?
➲ inside the setting or classroom (ensure that different parts of the setting are covered);
➲ in the outdoor play area;
➲ outside the classroom (if appropriate);
➲ in the hall or the playground (if appropriate).

When?
➲ before or after teaching;
➲ while working with the child/children;
➲ while child/children working independently;
➲ on adult-initiated or child-initiated activities.

Next you need to consider which is the most appropriate assessment technique to use to gather the evidence that you need. If it involves observation, you need to consider what kind of observation schedule or pro forma would be most appropriate. The National Numeracy Strategy provides an example of a feedback sheet to be used by other adults when working with and assessing children, which can be modified and adapted according to your needs. This is available in the training materials sent to schools.

Drummond (1996) stresses the need for practitioners to build observation and assessment into their everyday practice. She suggests that this is best achieved by recognising that they already have many of the required skills, that is the ability or *'power to think for themselves, to look for themselves and to act for themselves.'* (Drummond, 1996, page 111)

Using other kinds of observation schedules

In the last chapter you gained experience of carrying out observations on individual children. Now you are going to use a different schedule with a group of children and systematically analyse what the observation tells you about their development and learning.

Preparation
Select a group of children to observe either playing or working together.

Task
Observe the group of children for up to ten minutes and note relevant information on all the sections with the exception of the analysis of learning section which will be completed after the observation.

Group observation sheet	Children being observed
Date	Time
Place	Situation/context

Observation

Analysis of learning observed (to include all relevant areas of learning)

Action to be taken in relation to supporting children's development or extending their learning

Action to be taken in relation to providing different resources

Evaluation and follow up
Now take some time to consider very carefully what learning you have observed. Refer to the different areas of learning outlined within the Curriculum Guidance for the Foundation Stage, if necessary, to support you in this process. Make notes on this within the relevant section of the pro forma.

Think about the way the children were interacting with one another as well as the resources. Is there anything you have learned through this process that would inform the way you wish to work with them, either individually or as a group, in the future? Perhaps you might wish to provide different resources, which might also extend their learning or support their development in a particular way. If so, now try and organise a follow-up activity in which you implement any of the actions identified.

Review this action, and consider carefully what you have learned as a result of this process. Discuss this with other practitioners or adults working in the setting or classroom with you.

Involving children actively in their learning

Children need to be allowed to make some decisions about the learning activities in which they are engaged, what resources to use and how they might go about this. Reflecting on this process afterwards and learning as a result of that reflection is another important feature of involving children actively in their learning. This is a feature commonly adopted in early years settings that draw upon the High Scope model. Children are provided with a range of opportunities to direct their own learning and/or select what they wish to do from the activities available. An important aspect of this approach is to reflect upon and review what they have done, with adult support and, often, in front of their peers. For further reading on High Scope please refer to Hohman and Weikart (1995).

This process is also clearly linked to fostering independent thinkers and children who are self-motivated and not just reliant upon external reward systems. If this process is modelled and encouraged within a classroom or setting then children should move towards having a sense of ownership of their learning and a clear idea about how to proceed with their learning. In other words, what they might do or learn next. The following list of questions is adapted from Fisher (2002, page 192) and can be used to encourage young children to reflect on themselves as learners or on a particular activity, play experience or piece of work:

- ➲ Have I enjoyed playing with ...?
- ➲ Have I enjoyed doing ...?
- ➲ What have I found out or discovered?
- ➲ What do I enjoy doing?
- ➲ What do I want to do next?
- ➲ What helps me learn or play?
- ➲ Do I think I need help?
- ➲ Do I know who/how to go about getting help?
- ➲ What would I like to know?
- ➲ What can I tell someone about what I have discovered?

Preparation
Read the setting or school policy on assessment. Discuss this with those working in your setting and ask them how they try to involve children in self-assessment. Observe this, if possible.

Task
Consider how you might involve a small group of children (or one or two individuals) in some self-assessment. Build this into your planning and make clear to the children what you want them to think about. How are you going to organise, manage and lead this? Will you provide a model to the children of what you want them to consider or have this as a more open discussion? You may wish to use or adapt some of the questions identified in the section above. How will you ensure that each individual contributes to and gains from this process? Will the self-assessment focus on one activity or on a more general aspect of their learning? Keep a record of this process.

Evaluation and follow up
What have you learned about encouraging young children to reflect on their learning and how you can facilitate this? What might you consider integrating into your practice in relation to self- assessment on a more regular basis?

Linking assessment and planning

The planning cycle is the process by which practitioners identify and address children's developmental and learning needs based on formative assessment. Assessment can and should take place at the beginning and end of this cycle. At the beginning it will be focused on finding out what children already know, can do or understand. This information should then be used to make sure that the next learning experiences planned are meaningful and relevant to the child/children being taught. Indeed the dynamic relationship between assessment and planning is clearly indicated within the *Curriculum Guidance for the Foundation Stage*, which says that:

> '*Assessment gives insights into children's interests, achievements and possible difficulties in their learning from which next steps in learning and teaching can be planned.*' (QCA, 2000, page 24)

This document goes on to state that:

'Practitioners need to share information gained from assessment to:

⊃ *inform their future planning;*
⊃ *group children for particular activities and interests;*
⊃ *ensure that the curriculum meets the needs of all children;*
⊃ *promote continuity and progression.'*
(QCA, 2000 page 24)

An expanded version of this planning and assessment cycle could be used to highlight the detail of more formalised assessment practices. If it is appropriate, the teacher might record the assessments. These records can then be analysed and either used to report to parents or set suitable targets for the individual child, small groups of children or even the class. Target setting has become a significant issue particularly in schools, over the last few years. It has become common practice for practitioners and teachers to set SMART targets. Targets should be:

⊃ **S**pecific (tightly focused).
⊃ **M**easurable (able to be demonstrated and so using active verbs).
⊃ **A**chievable (the next small step).
⊃ **R**ealisable or realistic.
⊃ **T**ime related (achievable within an agreed time frame e.g. half a term).

Example: *Within a month, Jamil will indicate some form of response when he is addressed by name.*

These targets can then be built into future plans so that the children have a chance to work towards and then meet the targets. These targets should be written in simple language so that they can be shared with children as well as parents or carers. Young children will also need to be reminded about their targets at relevant points when they are working. This process exemplifies how assessments of different kinds (either formative or summative) should be used to inform teaching and learning.

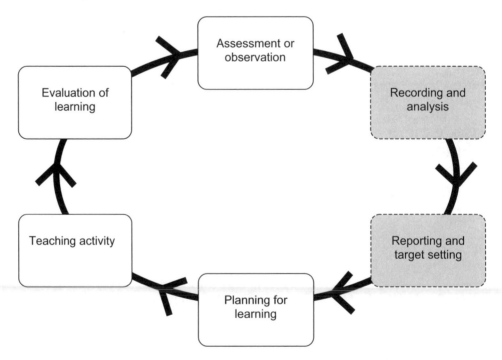

This diagram shows how the process of planning and assessment can be extended to include target setting. This extension to the process might be adopted for all children particularly in the areas of communication, language and literacy or mathematical development. However, it may also be used for children with special educational needs and linked to individual educational plans.

Your achievements

Now you have read this section and completed the activities you should be able to:

⊃ recognise the need to identify at the planning stage who will be assessing children, where and when;

⊃ carry out observations on groups of children;

⊃ analyse the development and learning needs of these children as a result of this observation;

⊃ decide how you might respond to support their development and learning;

⊃ be familiar with the setting or school assessment policy and implement this accordingly;

⊃ involve children in self-assessment, evaluate the success of this process and consider how to integrate this into your practice;

⊃ understand the relationship between assessment and planning and use this to support children's development and learning.

If you feel that you have completed the tasks successfully, return to the relevant needs analysis and mark it off with the date and evidence. If appropriate, ask your tutor about being able to use this as evidence of your understanding or professional capability. This information could be used as part of the course you are studying. This may be evidence towards the Professional Standards for QTS or it might be part of a profile or an assignment you might be completing as part of your studies. Please refer to the tables at the back of the book which detail coverage against the principles listed within the *Curriculum Guidance for the Foundation Stage* as well as the Professional Standards for QTS.

Making a contribution to the setting

Conclusion

Now that you have reached the end of this chapter you should feel confident that you can make a contribution to the work of the setting. You have had an opportunity to explore and practise some aspects of your professional knowledge, understanding and skills across all the themes covered. You should have a developing understanding of how young children learn, and of the ways in which you can plan and provide for, as well as support, learning and development for individuals and groups of children. It is essential that you check you have evidence to support all the statements in the appropriate needs analysis tables for this level. It is also important that you talk to your lead practitioner or school-based mentor at this stage. He or she will be able to help you check that you have appropriate evidence to audit your progress. If you are a trainee teacher you should also cross-reference this to the Professional Standards for QTS (see Appendix **page 129**) and start to complete the profiling required by your training provider. You are now ready to develop your own practice further and take greater responsibility for or within the setting.

Contents

The information and activities in this section are aimed at practitioners who have increasing responsibility for the work of the setting as a whole. This responsibility may include planning for learning throughout the setting, as well as teaching. At this stage in your professional development you may also find yourself planning for the deployment of other adults in the setting, and taking responsibility for the ongoing management and organisation of the team for much of the time. The expectation is that you have worked through all of the previous chapter, 'Making a contribution to the setting', and its activities. If you are a trainee teacher it is likely that you will be nearing the end of your training and completing an extended placement in a Foundation Stage setting.

The activities described in this chapter can be carried out in any Foundation Stage setting, and across the areas of learning outlined in the *Curriculum Guidance*. Foundation Stage settings are complex places and this chapter is designed to support you as you begin to get to know, and make sense of practice in the setting.

The *Curriculum Guidance for the Foundation Stage* identifies a number of principles which are '*drawn from, and are evident in, good and effective practice in early years settings*' (QCA, 2000 page 11). A summary of this book's coverage of the principles included in the *Curriculum Guidance* is given in an Appendix at the end of the book. It may be helpful to you to refer to this.

If you are training to be a teacher in the Foundation Stage you will need to audit your development by reference to the statements in *Qualifying to Teach Professional Standards for Qualified Teacher Status* (DfES/TTA, 2003), which set out what a trainee teacher must know, understand and be able to do to be awarded QTS. A summary of the Standards that are addressed by different themes is also included as an Appendix. Please refer to this regularly.

As you complete each piece of evidence that accompanies the activities it is important that you share this with your supervising practitioner, school based mentor, colleagues and/or tutor, as relevant to your situation. This profiling process is particularly important for trainee teachers, and your training provider should advise you on this. Do ensure that you link the completion of the activities in this chapter with the profiling requirements of your training.

The matrix below outlines the content and activities for this chapter. Use it to help you plan your further learning. If you are a trainee teacher use the summary of the Standards for the Award of Teacher Status to see how your experiences at this level can contribute directly to the profiling process.

	When finding out about policy and practice in the setting	When observing children	When observing other practitioners	When planning an activity, lesson or aspect of practice	When teaching an activity or lesson	When reflecting on your practice
Young children as learners and enquirers	Reread the early years policy for teaching and learning. Facilitate a discussion with the team about the theoretical underpinning/shared understanding of teaching and learning.				Ask a colleague to observe you working with children, focusing in particular on your use of questioning.	Reflect on your questioning and style of interaction with the children. How might you encourage thinking and positive attitudes and disposition to learning?
Making connections in children's learning		Observe the opportunities for children to engage in the expressive arts. Observe children's play to identify schemas.	Observe how adults interact with children to support children's self-expression.			Reflect on how you can nourish and support children's self-expression and schematic behaviour to take their thinking and learning further.
Adults and children working together	Identify opportunities to collaborate with parents and the wider community to support children's learning.		Observe, assess and evaluate the dimensions of children's learning taking account of the context, process and/or outcome of learning.	Plan an activity that involves parents or the wider community in children's learning. Carry out a risk assessment for a special event.		Evaluate the planning and reflect on how the event or activity could be improved. Reflect on the ways in which the adult contributions to the event were managed.
Organising the environment for learning	Facilitate a discussion with the team and the children about the use of materials and equipment. Model possible changes.					Reflect on what changes to the physical environment should be made, based on your discussions and modelling.
Planning for learning	Become familiar with the long-term planning for the setting. Read any related curriculum policies.				Devise a medium-term plan based on the long-term planning. Produce weekly plans based on the medium-term planning; consider observation/ assessment to include opportunities for child initiated activities.	Evaluate planning each week and use this information to inform future plans and opportunities for child initiated activities. Review your medium-term planning and reflect upon the planning process.
Observing and assessing young children	Investigate the procedures for gathering information about children before they join the setting. Become familiar with the systems in place for sampling, analysing and recording children's development or learning. Examine some Annual Reports to Parents completed by other practitioners.	Observe a child (or examine a piece of work) to identify which of the Stepping Stones or Early Learning Goals have been successfully demonstrated.		Plan a list of questions that you might ask a parent or carer to elicit important information before their child joins the setting. Discuss this with a colleague. Produce reports for parents of two children using the pro forma provided by the setting.		Reflect on your questions and the procedures in place to gather information about children, particularly the messages they convey to parents. Reflect on the process, analysing children's achievements and the changes that you might make to your practice.

All the activities in this chapter are outlined in full and have the following information provided with them:

➲ essential background to the activity, including the use of resources, and which context might be the most appropriate for carrying it out;
➲ suggested background reading;
➲ a description of the activity and all the elements that go to make it up;
➲ ideas on how to evaluate its success;
➲ your achievements.

Chapter 5   Young children as learners and enquirers

The preceding chapters have allowed you to develop your knowledge and understanding of how young children learn and how you as an early years practitioner can use theoretical knowledge to underpin your practice with young children. This section will build upon the theoretical discussion so far and will also enable you to address issues concerned with managing learning and teaching within a team approach.

The early years policy

QCA (2000) sums up the approach to learning and teaching in the final principle: *'above all, effective learning and development for young children requires high-quality care and education by practitioners'* (page 12). This can only be achieved if all members of the early years team have a shared understanding and expectations of how young children learn. Writing an early years policy which outlines beliefs about how young children learn and the teaching approach required to support children learning is a necessary first step. However, the policy must be discussed, debated and written by the team. You will have looked at working as a member of the early years team on **page 80**.

The process of developing the policy is as important as the policy itself. Discussion about how the team enables children to feel safe and secure and engage in active learning, for example, will develop and strengthen practice. Edgington (1998, Chapter 2) provides a useful framework and approach to developing an early years policy. An early years policy should include the following headings and issues.

Rationale
- Why do we need a distinctive approach to teaching young children?
- What do we believe about:
    - children;
    - how they learn;
    - an appropriate environment in which children can learn;
    - how we can best interact with and teach children;
- Why do we hold these beliefs?

Purposes or outcomes
- What do we want to achieve for young children?
- What do we want children to be doing?
- What do we want adults to be doing?

Broad guidelines
- How will we ensure our purposes are achieved?

Monitoring and evaluation
- How will we monitor and review this policy?
- Who will do this?
- When will it be done?

(Adapted from Edgington, 1998, page 37.)

In Chapter 3 you were asked to read the early years policy and now need to revisit this.

Preparation
- Reread the early years policy.
- Familiarise yourself with the above framework.
- Discuss with the team manager your approach to a team meeting, focusing on teaching and learning within the early years policy.
- Negotiate a team meeting to discuss the early years policy.

Task
Using information from your reading:

- With the team manager identify points for discussion related to teaching and learning and the early years policy. For example: How do we believe young children learn? Where do our beliefs come from? How can we be most effective in helping young children learn?
- Use the points to facilitate a meeting with the staff.
- Relate your discussion points to the current early years policy.

Evaluation and follow up
Reflect on your findings using the following questions:

- Is there shared understanding about how young children learn?
- Are there any differences in opinions?
- Is there a theoretical underpinning to team members understanding of how children learn?
- Is there a shared understanding about the most effective teaching approach?
- Are there any differences in opinions?
- How might these differences be resolved?
- How do your findings relate to the current early years policy?
- On reflection there might be a need for further discussion with the team manager and the team as well as amending the early years policy?

The learning needs of all children

The process of understanding how all children learn and how you as the teacher meet the needs of all children is an ongoing one. By now you have identified how young children learn using your increasing knowledge of child development and learning theories. To continue to develop your theoretical understanding you might like to read Greenfield (2001) who gives insights into brain development and how young children learn. You now need to consider some additional ways in which young children learn.

Preferred sensory systems

The work of Alistair Smith (1996) has shown us that individuals receive and process information in one of three preferred styles. These are:

- visual – learners who prefer to use pictures, diagrams, mind maps etc.;
- auditory – learners who prefer the spoken word, songs, rhymes, stories and music;
- kinaesthetic – learners who prefer to 'do' using role-play and practical activity.

Children in your class will potentially fall into one of these three groups. You need to consider in your planning, and that of the team, how you cater for all sensory styles in your teaching. You also need to consider the impact of your own sensory style when planning and teaching. For example, if your preferred style is auditory, is there a dominance of talking and using stories and rhyme in the activities you choose to teach? Planning and teaching as an early years team should ensure that different approaches are used and the range of sensory styles catered for. When you and the team evaluate the planning and teaching you need to consider the above issues.

Questioning

In the previous chapter open-ended questioning was identified as a key strategy in developing children's learning. Adult–child interactions, where both parties are involved in a dialogue and open-ended questions are used to encourage thinking and develop learning, entail what Siraj-Blatchford *et al.* (2002) call 'sustained shared thinking'. In their research they attest that effective early years practice must contain periods of sustained shared thinking between adults and children. As a part of your ongoing development as an early years practitioner you must reflect on and evaluate the use of your own questioning style and your interactions with children.

Preparation
Negotiate a time for your practitioner to observe you working with a small group with a particular focus on questioning.

Task
Ask the practitioner to record the questions you use and the responses given by the children. Ensure that all dialogue is recorded. You may find it useful for your practitioner to use the format given for the questioning task in the previous chapter.

Evaluation and follow up
With your practitioner analyse the transcript of your small group time. Note the type and the frequency of the questions used. Consider whether there were any periods of sustained shared thinking. Reflect upon and discuss how you might change aspects of your questioning style to encourage greater thinking and learning by the children. Also consider if your questioning and style of interaction encourages positive attitudes and dispositions in children.

Your achievements

Now you have read this section and completed the activities you should be able to:

➲ understand the importance of an effective early years policy;
➲ identify what makes an effective early years policy;
➲ understand the importance of a whole team understanding and approach to learning and teaching in the early years;
➲ recognise the importance of preferred sensory styles for children's learning;
➲ understand the influence of your own preferred sensory style on your teaching;
➲ evaluate your own questioning style and develop it to encourage interactions with children, which involve sustained shared thinking.

If you feel that you have completed the tasks successfully, return to the relevant needs analysis and mark it off with the date and evidence. If appropriate, ask your tutor about being able to use this as evidence of your understanding or professional capability. This information could be used as part of the course you are studying. This may be evidence towards the Professional Standards for QTS or it might be part of a profile or an assignment you might be completing as part of your studies. Please refer to the tables at the back of the book which detail coverage against the principles listed within the *Curriculum Guidance for the Foundation Stage* as well as the Professional Standards for QTS.

Making connections in children's learning

The status of play

In the previous chapters you have been introduced to some of the key issues concerned with children's play and you will have developed these ideas further through your reading. You will now be introduced to the debate concerning the status of play in early years settings.

Generally, early years practitioners understand the central role that play has in children's learning. However, within education overall, play has not been valued nor has it been given high status. If children are going to gain educational benefit from play then those working with young children must work together to raise the status of play so that everyone can understand the place of play in children's learning. Fisher (2002a) presents a Charter for Play, which may support practitioners in understanding, valuing and articulating the benefits of play. It may also support the early years team in developing a shared understanding of the importance and place of play in children's learning. Once this is achieved, consideration must be given to how you convince colleagues, parents and governors of the importance of play.

A Charter for Play

➲ *Acknowledge* its unique contribution as a process by which young children learn.
➲ *Plan* for it as an integral part of the curriculum and not an 'added extra'.
➲ *Facilitate* it with appropriate and high-quality provision.
➲ *Act* as a catalyst when intervention is appropriate and a scaffolder when expertise is required.
➲ *Observe* it in order to have first-hand evidence of children's learning.
➲ *Evaluate* it in order to better understand the needs of the learner.
➲ *Value* it through comment and commitment in order for its status in the classroom to be appreciated.
➲ *Fight* for it with rigorous, professional argument in order to bring about deeper understanding and acceptance by colleagues, parents, governors and the community at large (Fisher, 2002a, page 128).

Playful teaching

Another way of raising the status of play in settings is through evaluation of the adult role in play. Adults need to observe children at play, provide a challenging environment for children's play and plan for play but they must also involve themselves in children's play. Moyles (1994) shows that the value of play can be derived from the implicit messages sent through adult engagement in play. Adults who involve themselves in children's play send powerful and positive messages about the status of play. Moyles and Adams (2001) discuss the necessity for playful teaching and outline scenarios where adults join in with children's play.

Creative teaching

Supporting and promoting children's creativity involves practitioners in being creative themselves. Duffy (1998) discusses two approaches to the adult role in children's creativity:

➲ non-interventionist – not being directly involved;
➲ interventionist – being involved to develop children's creativity.

Historically, there has been a view that direct adult intervention can destroy the flow of children's creativity. However, as discussed on **page 8** theorists such as Vygotsky and Bruner have emphasised the importance of the adult role in children's learning and the adult role is also crucial in developing children's creativity. Adults need to create an environment in which children want to be creative and imaginative and in which they interact sensitively with children to develop creativity and imagination. Adults also need to make connections between children's creative and imaginative play activities and their overall development.

The Reggio Emilia approach to early years education is one where creativity, play, communication and collaboration are emphasised. In this approach, making connections in their learning is crucial for both adults and children. In order to develop greater understanding and knowledge of this important approach to early years education read Edwards *et al.* (1998) or Abbott and Nutbrown (2001).

All our languages

One aspect of the Reggio Emilia approach to early years education mentioned above is the focus on all the expressive languages used by children to represent their thoughts and feelings. The approach also emphasises that adults should listen to each other as well. By listening to children communicating in different ways and to each other, true collaboration and meaning can be achieved. Working as a team and listening to each other has been addressed (**page 80**). In this section you will focus on children communicating in ways other than linguistic. Within the Reggio Emilia approach verbal discussion is seen as the centrepiece to negotiations and working together but other ways of children expressing themselves are also powerful (Malaguzzi in Edwards *et al.* 1998). Other ways that children can express themselves include:

- ⊃ drawing;
- ⊃ painting;
- ⊃ sculpture;
- ⊃ making sounds;
- ⊃ music;
- ⊃ dance;
- ⊃ puppetry;
- ⊃ shadows;
- ⊃ photography;
- ⊃ information and communications technology.

Also in this approach children and adults work collaboratively on a shared project, which enables children and adults to play with ideas, communicate, imagine and create. In sum, this approach truly offers children and adults who work together, the opportunity to make connections in children's learning. Working in this way requires commitment and belief by all members of the early years team. However, it is possible to evaluate the opportunities that you provide for children to express themselves in different ways.

Preparation
Prepare to observe children and adults working together over a week. Your focus will be on the opportunities children have for expressing themselves and how adults work with children in this process.

Task
Carry out your observations at times convenient to you and the rest of the team.

Use the following table to help you organise your observations. You may add to the list of opportunities for children to engage in the expressive arts, as these will be unique to your setting.

Opportunities	Evidence
Painting	
Drawing	
Modelling	
Building	
Music	
Dance	
Puppets	

Evaluation and follow up

Reflect on and evaluate your observations using the following questions:

- ➲ What is the range of opportunities given to children to express themselves?
- ➲ Is there an overemphasis on some types of activities?
- ➲ Are there missed opportunities for children to express themselves?
- ➲ How could you introduce further opportunities for children to communicate using the expressive arts?
- ➲ How do adults in the setting respond to children's communications?
- ➲ How are children's communications shared with parents?

You may wish to share and discuss your findings with the team.

Schema

In Chapter 2 you were introduced to the concept of schemas. In this chapter you will begin to identify the types of schematic behaviour that young children demonstrate. Paffard in Smidt (1998) outlines a schema spotter's guide, which identifies many of the different schematic behaviours, which children may use. Below are some of the common schemas seen in children's behaviour with a brief description to aid identification. (For a more comprehensive guide read Paffard in Smidt (1998), Chapter 24.)

Transporting
A child will move items from place to place using a bag or trolley.

Trajectory
The child likes to see things moving through the air. This may be balls or hoops. It may also be expressed through the physical actions of the child by throwing, jumping or kicking.

Vertical or horizontal
A child may like to move up and down or horizontally. Objects may be placed in lines, or moved in vertical or horizontal directions. Paintings may consist of vertical or horizontal lines.

Circularity
As above, but the fascination will be in a circular direction.

Enclosing
A child may build enclosures with blocks and bricks. Sometimes the enclosure is empty or it may be filled in. Paintings may have an enclosing line painted around them.

Enveloping
This is an extension of enclosing. Space, objects or the child may be covered. Spaces may be enclosed; for example building dens. Objects may be wrapped up and the child may enjoy dressing up or playing under covers.

However, it is not enough to simply identify children's individual schematic behaviour. Once a schema has been identified it is necessary to provide a range of experiences, which extend the child's thinking along that schematic path.

Example: *Jack exhibits a trajectory schema and is always throwing objects as well as moving himself in different trajectories. Janet, the nursery nurse develops a range of activities to support his behaviour as well as extend his skills and knowledge of different aspects of the curriculum. Activities include:*

- *throwing balls into numbered buckets;*
- *filling plastic syringes with paint and squirting it at paper;*
- *rolling wheeled toys down different inclines;*
- *kicking balls into goals;*
- *experimenting with yo-yos;*
- *making and testing paper aeroplanes;*
- *a visit to the airport to watch the planes.*

Preparation
Observe four children at different play activities over a week.

Task
Observe the children playing at different activities and make notes on their behaviours. If you can identify a particular schema introduce specific resources and activities to nourish their schematic behaviour.

Evaluation and follow up
Reflect upon and evaluate your findings using the following questions:

- Were you able to identify specific schema?
- Did individual children exhibit more than one schema?
- How did they respond to the additional resources?
- How did they respond to the additional activities?
- Were other children interested in the additional resources and activities?
- How might you take their learning and thinking further?

You may wish to share your knowledge of the children's schematic behaviour with the parents and the rest of the team to develop your own knowledge and understanding of the children further.

Your achievements

Now you have read this section and completed the activities you should be able to:

- understand the need to raise the status of play in settings;
- understand your own role in raising the status of play through discussion and working with children;
- identify an appropriate adult role in developing children's creativity;
- have some knowledge and understanding of the Reggio Emilia approach to early years education;
- identify a variety of ways in which children can communicate using all their expressive languages;
- identify common schemas in children's behaviour;
- support and extend children's schematic behaviour through appropriate intervention.

If you feel that you have completed the tasks successfully, return to the relevant needs analysis and mark it off with the date and evidence. If appropriate, ask your tutor about being able to use this as evidence of your understanding or professional capability. This information could be used as part of the course you are studying. This may be evidence towards the Professional Standards for QTS or it might be part of a profile or an assignment you might be completing as part of your studies. Please refer to the tables at the back of the book which detail coverage against the principles listed within the *Curriculum Guidance for the Foundation Stage* as well as the Professional Standards for QTS.

Adults and children working together

You have developed a good understanding of the different partnerships in the setting, the roles and responsibilities of the immediate team and the collaboration between that team, parents and carers, the community and the wider range of professionals whose services complement them and enhance the children's opportunities to express themselves and learn. In the *Curriculum Guidance for the Foundation Stage* emphasis is placed on these relationships in the section relating to personal, social and emotional development: *'to give all children the best opportunities for personal, social and emotional development, practitioners should give particular attention to establishing constructive relationships with children, with other practitioners, between practitioners and children, with parents and with workers from other agencies, that take account of differences and different needs and expectations' (QCA, 2000, page 28).*

Introduction

In this section you will look in more detail at team building, medium-term planning and identifying opportunities for collaborating with parents and the local community to enrich the experiences of the children. In the section on 'Planning for learning' in this chapter you will explore further the nature of medium-term planning and have some involvement in the medium-term planning process (see page 112).

Team building

As a practitioner, it may be your responsibility to lead and develop the team, or some aspect of it. Edgington (1998) describes the complexity of this role:

'Being a leader makes many different demands on the nursery teacher, depending on the other adults they are involving in their work … Leadership does not just involve telling people what to do or leading from the front. For the nursery teacher is also involves befriending, explaining, supporting, respecting, valuing, enabling, partnering, listening, including coordinating, cooperating and sharing.' (Edgington, 1998, page 4)

She goes on to analyse the aspects of leadership and the elements needed to achieve a task:

➲ clarifying principles which underpin the provision;
➲ defining the tasks by developing the policies and practices of the setting;
➲ breaking down the tasks, by prioritising and ensuring that plans are achievable and not overwhelming; this also means involving the team in prioritising;
➲ team building by involving others, ensuring shared understanding and seeking commitment;
➲ co-ordination and communication by acting as a link between team members and between the team and others;
➲ developing individuals by knowing them well and appraising their work;
➲ delegating responsibility, by allowing others to use their skills within the agreed philosophical framework.

For a detailed discussion of this analysis see Edgington (1998, Chapter 1).

Observation of the learning environment and other adults

The work of Pascal and Bertram through the Effective Early Learning Research Project (1996) has already been mentioned in Chapter 2. Their work focused on three key areas: the context, process and outcome. It might be helpful to refer back to their work at this stage or to read about it in more detail (see Pascal and Bertram, 1996). One key aspect that needs to be addressed relates to how practitioners can evaluate the context of the learning environment and use this information to make appropriate changes. This has been covered on **page 110**. This must also take into account the dynamic between the children and the adults. This aspect of the early years setting is explored by Pascal and Bertram through two different observation schedules: the adult engagement schedule and the adult supportive intervention scale. It is highly recommended for all practitioners to familiarise themselves with the principles underlining these schedules and details about the information they can provide.

Preparation and task
Use the schedule below or aspects of it to evaluate one or all of the three dimensions covered i.e. context, process or outcome within the setting in which you are working. Refer to **page 36** for definitions of the terms. Keep notes as evidence of responses to the questions. It might be helpful to enlarge the schedule and write notes alongside each question.

Evaluation and follow up
Review what you have learned as a result of systematically answering some of the questions in the table. What changes might you instigate in your own practice or that of the setting in which you are working as a result of this analysis? Devise a simple action plan for yourself, to address or improve one or more aspect identified as a result of this exercise. This may be set out as below.

Area to be addressed	Action to be taken	Review period	Evidence of change

Initiatives that support families

Sure Start
In 1999 the government introduced the Sure Start programme (DfEE, 1999a): *'This programme was designed to offer comprehensive support to families with children under four in disadvantaged neighbourhoods. A Sure Start Unit accountable to both the Minister for Health and the Minister for Education was set up. Identified communities were invited to prepare proposals for innovative multidisciplinary work ... and there was an expectation that local people would be involved in developing local bids.'* (Whalley, 2001, page 7). The Sure Start programme has developed substantially since its introduction. For up-to-date information on the latest provision refer to the website at www.surestart.org.uk

Family Literacy and Numeracy
Family Literacy and Family Numeracy are also initiatives set up by central government. They are aimed at breaking down intergenerational literacy and numeracy problems. Families are invited to take part in a series of workshops, in school and during school time. Qualified teachers work with the children and trained tutors work with the parents. After the separate sessions the two groups come together and work collaboratively.

Parenting classes and workshops
Many Foundation Stage settings organise classes and workshops for parents. These may be led by the staff within the setting, or by one of the professionals described in Chapter 4, **page 79**.

Example: *During the regular exchange of news and information at the end of the morning session in the nursery, Tanveer, the nursery teacher is talking to two mothers and telling them how well their sons, Iqbal and Jason, play together, share equipment and enjoy a similar sense of humour. The mothers both say behaviour is not like that at home. Tanveer says that they may be interested in coming to a series of forthcoming sessions entitled, 'Coping with Kids', which will be led by Tim, an advisory teacher in the Department of Education. The mothers say 'Put our names on the list now'.*

Visits and outings

Involving the local community in the work of the setting may involve taking children on visits and outings. Before undertaking an event such as this you must analyse the potential risks involved. Local education authorities and schools will have guidelines for making a risk assessment, and these must be followed explicitly.

Preparation

Look at the medium-term planning for the next few weeks.

Task

Look at the medium-term planning task later in this chapter. Plan an activity involving visitors such as the senior citizen's club at the community centre or an outing for the children. Refer to the task in 'Planning for learning' (Chapter 5, **page 114**). Look for opportunities to involve parents and the wider community. Make a risk assessment if this is required for the activity you plan. Think about the skills the children will be using and acquiring whilst preparing for and participating in the visit. For example: Helping to make invitations, planning and helping to prepare food, preparing and practicing songs, music, dances, talking about their perceptions and experiences of old people.

Think about the staff in the setting and how they will contribute in particular to the event.

Make a table of the tasks which may be involved.

Key consideration	Notes	Particular staff or helpers involved	Who is responsible for organising?
Risk assessment			
Permission			
Supervision or adult assistance needed			
Preparation of children			
Special clothing if any			
Special equipment or resources if any			
Information for parents			
Invitations if any			
Finance or costs			
Transport arrangements if any			
First aid arrangements if different from usual			
Follow up			

Evaluation and follow up

Evaluate the planning. Was it adequate? Was the event successful for the participants? What were the strengths of the individual team members and of the other adults who helped and were these strengths suited to the particular tasks assigned to them? How could you improve a similar event in the future?

Your achievements

Now you have read this section and completed the activities you should be able to:

⊃ understand the importance of building an effective Foundation Stage team;
⊃ be aware of some team building strategies;
⊃ understand the nature of multidisciplinary work in Foundation Stage settings;
⊃ observe and evaluate the contributions of other adults to the learning environment;
⊃ consider how to use this information to change an aspect of practice within the setting;
⊃ be aware of the ways in which schools support parents and families;
⊃ plan an activity which involves parents and the wider community, undertaking a risk assessment where necessary;
⊃ evaluate activities involving parents.

If you feel that you have completed the tasks successfully, return to the relevant needs analysis and mark it off with the date and evidence. If appropriate, ask your tutor about being able to use this as evidence of your understanding or professional capability. This information could be used as part of the course you are studying. This may be evidence towards the Professional Standards for QTS or it might be part of a profile or an assignment you might be completing as part of your studies. Please refer to the tables at the back of the book which detail coverage against the principles listed within the *Curriculum Guidance for the Foundation Stage* as well as the Professional Standards for QTS.

You are now ready to work with your team and children to discuss changes and to provide information for parents and other colleagues about new ideas for the organisation of your learning environment.

Early years practitioners need to think about managing the environment for learning in ways that suit everybody. Time needs to be given to listening to children's views about space and time and to involving children in change. The tasks in Chapters 3 and 4 have allowed you to reflect on the organisation and the context of the environment. You have observed generally and recorded your observations. Look back at the observation tasks and consider how much you understand from them about the effect of the indoor and the outdoor environment on children's learning. You should now be able to move forward into an exciting programme of modification of the use of space and the provision of resources that takes into consideration children's independence, interests and dispositions and the way in which these complement curriculum aims for the Foundation Stage.

Transforming the environment

Before embarking on change it is important to reconsider the purpose of the learning environment. Rinaldi (1992) when talking about the Reggio Emilia tradition, considers that *'the best environment for children is one where the quality and the quantity of relationships is as high as possible.'* (Cited in Cadwell, 1997, page 93). By this she means, relationships between people, children, materials, and ideas. Gandini (1998, page 162 in Edwards *et al.* 1998) says that we can *'improve our ability to analyse deeper layers of meaning if we observe the extent to which everyone involved (in the environment) is at ease and how everyone uses the space itself.'* Curtis (1998, page 102) talks about contrasting environments. Two classrooms may be equipped in a similar manner with one offering children challenge and *'with opportunities for learning and discovery maximised'* and another with an overwhelming organisation of materials and little learning taking place.

Making changes within the environment

Carrying out changes in the learning environment requires reflection on the existing structure and ensuring that the team members understand the need for change. All early years settings have established an ethos for the use of space and the deployment of resources that reflects personal preferences and ongoing local and national influences of the type discussed in Chapter 2. Changes will be traumatic for some people and invigorating for others. It will generally be worthwhile if changes bring about a more harmonious and purposeful working environment. As a result of changing the learning environment you may be able to observe changes in children's learning and behaviour within the setting.

For example they may now:

⮕ choose from the full range of graphic materials when representing because the painting, drawing and writing areas are adjacent;
⮕ develop better imaginary play in the block area because additional resources such as cardboard boxes have been added;
⮕ play in role more frequently as there is now easy access to dressing up materials and items for domestic play;
⮕ use water and sand more creatively because equipment generally reserved for structured science activities has been made available;
⮕ access all materials easily because of improved storage facilities and careful grouping and organisation.

Such changes can encourage children to be more independent and creative learners.

Preparation
Edgington (1998) in Chapter 1 considers the complex issues of leading the team. She then goes on to consider aspects of implementing change. You and your team must be clear about why you think that changes to the environment are necessary. Your evidence will have been gathered from the tasks in Chapters 3 and 4.

Meetings with other team members will normally take place on a regular basis. Discussion of the learning environment should take place in these meetings. You have already shared observations and reflections. It is now time to work out how the environment can be developed in the short-term and how it can be continually reconsidered and revised in the longer term.

Consider the conclusions from the tasks in Chapter 3. You may agree to consider the physical environment only at this stage and return to the role of the adults at a later stage.

Task
Make a large plan or a model of the working space, both inside and outside. Make diagrams or use artefacts to represent key features i.e. fixtures, furniture and fittings. Introduce the children to the use of plans and models and discuss, with reference to the real situation around them, ways in which the environment might be changed. Use the plan/model and the artefacts for small scale practical demonstration and have ongoing discussion tempered with action! Put some of the changes in place as soon as possible and involve adults and children in making the physical moves to put changes into effect. Put the plan on the wall or the model on a table and draw parents' attention to it.

Evaluation and follow up
Observe, discuss and evaluate these changes with colleagues and children.

⮕ Are children using materials and equipment differently?
⮕ Are these changes helping children to learn actively and effectively?
⮕ Are they more independent?
⮕ Are areas of the setting being used differently and if so how?

The task in this theme may have inspired you to consider the environment for learning more seriously. Young children will learn when they are happy and when they encounter activities and requests that make sense to them. Their learning will move forward when they achieve a balance of adult-directed and child initiated opportunities and where play is recognised as an important way of allowing them to demonstrate their interests and stage of development and to move their learning forward in all areas of learning.

Your achievements

Now you have read this section and completed the activities you should be able to:

⮕ be confident in working with others to modify the learning environment;
⮕ understand how provision can be made for children's differing needs;
⮕ understand how to provide for well planned and purposeful activity both inside and outside;
⮕ work with the team to develop independent experiences where children are able to think for themselves;
⮕ maintain ongoing discussion about the effectiveness of the environment with the team and the children and respond to their suggestions.

If you feel that you have completed the tasks successfully, return to the relevant needs analysis and mark it off with the date and evidence. If appropriate, ask your tutor about being able to use this as evidence of your understanding or professional capability. This information could be used as part of the course you are studying. This may be evidence towards the Professional Standards for QTS or it might be part of a profile or an assignment you might be completing as part of your studies. Please refer to the tables at the back of the book which detail coverage against the principles listed within the *Curriculum Guidance for the Foundation Stage* as well as the Professional Standards for QTS.

By this stage in your training you will have become more confident about planning lessons and sequences of lessons for groups of children. You will also have planned and taught activities for all the children in the setting or class, such as story telling or circle time. You now need to develop your skill in planning for all the areas of learning over the medium-term, a period of time of about half a term, and responding to child initiated activities in your planning.

It is the medium-term planning which ensures that the curriculum provided has continuity, that there is progression in the activities and the children are able to make links in their learning. Although the *Curriculum Guidance for the Foundation Stage* provides the framework for planning, the detail may draw on other sources of information including published materials, whole setting or school schemes of work and materials provided by local education authorities. Look again at the example medium-term plan on **page 26** and at examples of past medium-term planning from your own setting.

Planning with and for the team

In Chapter 2, **page 28**, you were introduced to the notion of teacher intensive and teacher initiated activities. The balance between these has implications for the deployment of the adults in the team. As the lead practitioner, you will carry key responsibility for the medium and short-term planning. It is likely that the planning will be undertaken collaboratively, but it is your responsibility to make decisions regarding the deployment of other adults in the team, although you would be wise to discuss these issues with your more experienced colleagues. The issues involved in working with a team are explored in more detail on **page 80**.

One of the most important aspects of planning is to consider how the adults in the team will share the various learning activities and roles. Some of this will depend on the procedures in place in the setting, where staff may have an identified group of children that they work with for some of the time. Other decisions will be based on individual staff members' particular interests and expertise.

When planning you need to consider how you will teach as well as what you will be teach:

> 'Good planning is essential for ensuring a broad balanced and purposeful curriculum. As well as identifying what children should learn, curriculum plans also need to take account of how it is intended the teaching and learning will take place.' (QCA, 1997, page 5)

Brailsford, Hetherington and Abram (1999) provide a good summary of the various ways in which the adults in the setting can plan their teaching and intervention. Although this is explored in the context of language and literacy, the planned interventions could apply to any area of learning.

Roles of the adult in the nursery	
Supplying	Providing the resources necessary for children to develop their language and literacy skills.
Supporting	Helping children to achieve their aims by intervening sensitively when appropriate.
Scaffolding	Providing a framework for children so that they can achieve with help what they may not be able to do on their own tomorrow.
Sharing	Sharing ideas, thoughts and experiences with children. Sharing books with children. Making literacy a social activity.
Showing	Providing a role model for children. Demonstrating ways of doing things.
Saying	Giving feedback to children on their language and literacy achievements. Helping them develop the metacognitive skills necessary to analyse and discuss their own development.
Seeing	Observing children's development closely in order to plan effectively for their future development. Assessing their needs sensitively.

(Brailsford, Hetherington and Abram in Marsh and Hallet, 1999, page 195)

It is important to bear in mind when planning the ways in which the adults' actions will be directed towards supporting children's learning. As the lead practitioner in the team you will need to be aware of the skills and experience of your colleagues and plan their deployment to ensure that skills and expertise are used effectively. Different members of the team have different responsibilities, roles and interests and when planning you should aim to use these to the maximum benefit of the children.

Planning in mixed age classes: Reception and Year 1

The Foundation Stage documentation is designed to meet the needs of young learners and from the age from three to the end of the Reception year. You may find yourself in a mixed Reception/Year 1 class. In this situation, the curriculum for the younger children will be planned from the Foundation Stage guidance, whilst teaching for older pupils will be covered by the requirements of the National Curriculum and National Literacy and Numeracy Strategies. Planning to meet these complex needs is a challenge. In this situation you have to draw on both sets of documentation so that learning objectives for shared teaching activities are appropriate for Reception and Year 1 children. The following is an example. In geography, the teacher is covering recognition of the physical features in their locality from the National Curriculum with the Year 1 children. This relates well to observing, finding out about and identifying features in the place they live from the 'knowledge and understanding of the world' strand of the Foundation guidance. The teacher is therefore able to plan activities that cover learning objectives for children in both age groups.

On another occasion she wishes to plan from the 'physical development' area of learning, with a focus on the importance of keeping healthy. This provides an opportunity to plan part of the science requirements of the Key Stage 1 National Curriculum for the older children in the class.

Where it is possible to make links between the *Curriculum Guidance for the Foundation Stage* and the National Curriculum the planning for a mixed age class can reflect appropriate activities. However, where it is not possible to make coherent links between the two curricula it is much better to plan separately for the two age groups, and arrange the teaching of the groups accordingly.

Planning in mixed age classes: nursery and Reception

It is not common, but some settings include children aged three to five plus, perhaps in a joint nursery/Reception class. In this situation all of the children are within the Foundation Stage and so the planning will be based on the Curriculum guidance for this stage. However, the children are likely to be at a range of different starting points, and so the planning will need to differentiate carefully to meet these needs.

National Literacy and Numeracy Strategies

In mixed age classes and in some Reception settings, the National Literacy and Numeracy Strategies will be the basis of language and mathematics teaching. The strategies may be implemented in full or in a modified form. National guidance has been issued on planning for literacy and numeracy in the Reception class (DfEE, 2000). Where the literacy hour and daily mathematics lesson are taught in their entirety, in Reception classes, you will need to ensure that the content and structure is appropriate for children in the Foundation Stage. Recent official guidance on medium-term planning for literacy (DfES, 2003) extends the scope of the national Strategy to the beginning of the Foundation Stage. This guidance refers to the Foundation Stage as two age ranges: earlier Foundation Stage for children in nursery and later for Reception. It could be argued that this conflicts with the *Curriculum Guidance for the Foundation Stage*, which does not make a specific separation between nursery and Reception, referring only to the Foundation Stage as a developmental continuum. Whatever materials or guidance you use to support your planning you must ensure that the planning is based on the needs of the children in your care and the resources, activities and organisation is suited to their developmental stage.

Planning for equal opportunities

'Young children learn by making connections between their understanding and their experience. It is important that their experience in the learning environment reflects their cultural and religious experience, so that they are able to make links between home, community and nursery or school' (QCA, page 84). In addition, you should ensure that your planning does not reinforce damaging or limiting gender stereotypes, so that both boys and girls have access to a wide range of appropriate learning experiences. Increasingly, children who have Special Educational Needs are fully included in mainstream settings, rather than being educated separately, so curriculum planning will need to take account of the diverse needs of all the children in the setting. Some children with Special Educational Needs will receive support from other visiting staff such as speech or occupational therapists. You will find that these staff can make a valuable contribution to the planning and their ideas and expertise will help you provide access to an appropriate curriculum for children with special needs of any kind. Likewise, you may well find that LEA support staff, or members of the community in which the school is placed will help you learn more about the cultural and faith backgrounds of the children you are teaching. In this way you can develop your knowledge of the educational, cultural and faith backgrounds of your pupils and use this understanding to inform your planning. The importance of building strong partnerships with supporting professionals and community members is discussed in more detail in Chapter 4, **page 79**.

Preparation
Look at the long-term planning for the period you are in the class or setting. Read any related curriculum policies. Discuss with the lead practitioner any factors or issues that might affect how the long-term plans will be interpreted in the medium-term.

Task
Look again at the example of medium-term planning in Chapter 2, **page 26**. Using a similar outline, produce a medium-term plan for the period you are covering. Identify how you will observe or assess children's current level of understanding in these areas. Observation and assessment is discussed in more detail in the following section. Where possible, identify potential opportunities for child initiated activities. Discuss your plan with your teacher and with the team in the setting. Respond to any comments they may have.

Having completed your medium-term overview, produce a more detailed plan for the first week. Make sure that your weekly plan has clear learning objectives, differentiated activities, and includes plans for the deployment of adults in the setting. The headings which should be included on the weekly plan and a suggested outline are given on **page 27**.

Evaluation and follow up

At the end of your first week, evaluate the children's learning and review the remainder of your medium-term plan. Discuss this with the rest of the team and make changes to the plan. Think in particular about opportunities for child initiated activities, and how the plan can be developed to included these.

Your achievements

Now that you have read this section and completed the activities you should be able to:

➲ understand that planning should identify adult intervention in children's learning;
➲ recognise the complexity of planning in mixed age classes;
➲ recognise the importance of responding to children's experience, cultural, linguistic and faith backgrounds in your planning;
➲ complete medium-term planning based on the areas of learning;
➲ undertake weekly planning drawn from your medium-term planning.

If you feel that you have completed the tasks successfully, return to the relevant needs analysis and mark it off with the date and evidence. If appropriate, ask your tutor about being able to use this as evidence of your understanding or professional capability. This information could be used as part of the course you are studying. This may be evidence towards the Professional Standards for QTS or it might be part of a profile or an assignment you might be completing as part of your studies. Please refer to the tables at the back of the book which detail coverage against the principles listed within the *Curriculum Guidance for the Foundation Stage* as well as the Professional Standards for QTS.

Chapter 5   Observing and assessing young children

This section will enable you to extend and deepen your understanding of the assessment, monitoring and record keeping process so that you develop a coherent approach to this within your own practice. You will have the opportunity to reflect upon the role and nature of the records that need to be kept within a Foundation Stage setting in order to:

➲ find out about and monitor the progress of individuals;
➲ inform planning and provision and the constant evaluation of this;
➲ enable communication with other relevant parties (such as children, parents, colleagues, other professionals and LEAs).

What kind of records do I need to keep?

It is important to bear in mind at this stage how the evidence gained from your assessments will be recorded so that it can be shared with other practitioners, parents and the children.

Formative records
Formative records need to be kept in order to provide ongoing information about a child's progress and attainment. Having this information easily available should ensure that practitioners take account of it when planning and therefore devise activities which are purposeful, developmentally appropriate and enriching for all the children in their care. These records need to cover all the different areas of learning that are indicated in the *Curriculum Guidance for the Foundation Stage* (see QCA, 2002). These are:

➲ personal, social and emotional development;
➲ communication, language and literacy;
➲ mathematical development;
➲ knowledge and understanding of the world;
➲ physical development;
➲ creative development.

However, they may also include contributions from the child, parents or carers as well as other adults who work with the child. These records need to reflect all aspects of the child in terms of their development and learning as a 'whole being'. This is usually achieved through profiling, which is designed to gather evidence of a child's progress and achievement over time. Profiles need to contain:

➲ information gathered to support transitions (e.g. between home and the setting or school, or nursery and school);
➲ examples of children's work or achievements (including photographs), with dates, comments or annotations that provide some information about the context for the work;
➲ observations on children and interpretations of these observations by practitioners;
➲ comments from parents about their children's interests, feelings etc.;
➲ comments by the child that indicate their own feelings and reflections about what they have been doing.

It is good practice to make incidental notes of interesting things that the children say and do, as part of this data gathering process. However, it is really only significant achievements or moments which need to be recorded, otherwise the detail gained from these ongoing assessments would become too complex and unmanageable for most practitioners. However, there is no point in keeping any of this information if it does not directly inform future planning.

Egersdorff (2002, page 153) has provided a helpful list of questions that can be used by practitioners to decide whether achievements are significant and should be recorded.

➲ The child has demonstrated a skill for the first time.
➲ You feel the child has consolidated a concept after demonstrating proficiency on several occasions.
➲ The child has demonstrated clear understanding of a process, perhaps as a result of a problem-solving activity.
➲ The achievement may be significant for one particular child and should be defined for that child. For example, a child with speech and language difficulties may initiate a conversation with his peers for the first time.

It involves talking with children about their achievements. Do they feel these are significant too?

If it is truly a significant achievement, there will be implications for the planning of future teaching and learning opportunities for that child.

This information should allow practitioners to monitor the continuity of the provision being offered to the child and take account of the fact that children will often be in a variety of pre-school settings, including being at home. These observations and assessments on children should ensure that all those involved in the child's care are communicating with one another and therefore making helpful connections in the child's day-to-day experiences, which will support their development and learning.

Preparation

A number of Foundation Stage settings take the opportunity to visit parents, carers and children in their home setting prior to them starting in the new setting or school. This can be a valuable opportunity to observe the child in familiar circumstances as well as enable the practitioner to talk to the parents or carers about their child. The information gathered can then be used to ensure that the child has a smooth transition from one setting to another.

Discuss with other practitioners what systems are in place to gather this kind of information in the setting in which you are working. Also, try to find out about any other systems that they have experienced, perhaps in another context, which can be used in a similar way to gather important information. Try to analyse these different systems in terms of their advantages or disadvantages.

Task

Consider the information that you think would be important to gather prior to a child starting in a Foundation Stage setting. Write down a list of questions that you could ask a parent or carer in order to elicit this information.

Evaluation and follow up

Discuss the list of questions you have generated with your mentor or a colleague. Compare your list with any questions/documents/systems which are already used to gather this information in the setting in which you are currently working. Explore and evaluate any differences between these lists/systems with other practitioners. Try to ensure that you have also considered what messages these systems convey to parents about the contribution they have to make to their child's ongoing learning and development and whether this is being valued or not.

Summative records

It is also necessary to have summative assessment and record keeping systems. The intention of this is to summarise a child's achievements at a particular point in time and add rigour to the assessment process. These are generally more structured and systematic tracking systems where significant information is recorded across the six areas of learning identified within the *Curriculum Guidance for the Foundation Stage*. This information may take the form of analysing or levelling the evidence collected from a child using the Stepping Stones or Early Learning Goals within the *Curriculum Guidance for the Foundation Stage* (QCA, 2000) in order identify exactly where a child is in their learning and development, as supported by the evidence. It will also take the form of the Foundation Profile, which requires practitioners to assess children against all the different learning areas at the end of the Foundation Stage. Although this needs to be based on a practitioner's ongoing observations and assessment it will summarise each child's typical developments and achievements so that these can be recorded on assessment scales derived from the Stepping Stones or Early Learning Goals. There is detailed guidance provided to support those completing these profiles, which consists of a handbook, supporting video and CD-ROM. Information about this is also available from the QCA website www.qca.org.uk/ca/foundation. There are 13 assessment scales, each of which has nine points:

The first three points describe a child who is still progressing towards the Early Learning Goals and are based mainly on the Stepping Stones.

The next five points are drawn from the Early Learning Goals and sequenced *approximately* in order of difficulty but this might not reflect individual children's achievements. (*It is worth noting at this point that many early years practitioners will dispute the order of this list and find its very construction highly questionable, given the fact that young children develop and learn in all sorts of ways.*)

The final point in each scale describes a child who has achieved all the other points and is working consistently beyond the Early Learning Goals.

The guidance suggests that the practitioner must record each item that the child has achieved in each scale and each point needs to be considered separately. The information from these profiles should be used to report to parents at the end of the Foundation Stage and will also be collected formally by LEAs. It will also be passed on to the next teacher, along with any other internal records or profiles that have been collated.

Preparation

Find out what systems are in place within your setting for sampling, analysing and recording children's development and learning. Review several examples of how this has been completed for different children, across the learning areas. Note the kind of comments that are made about the context for the work and any other conventions used to annotate or record this information. Bear this information in mind when completing the following task and adapt it if necessary so that it is consistent with the expectations within your own setting.

Task

Choose a piece of work, (which could be a photograph or tape recording) or decide to observe a child and analyse a significant learning experience. Now identify which area(s) of learning is evidenced by this work. Write down relevant annotations or comments about the context within which the learning took place. Then refer to the detailed information provided on the Stepping Stones or Early Learning Goals within the Curriculum Guidance for the Foundation Stage (QCA, 2000) and try to identify which of these have been successfully demonstrated through this piece of work or achievement. Note this clearly on the back of the work or using the appropriate record sheet.

Evaluation and follow up

Now show the evidence, your comments/annotations and analysis to another practitioner working in the setting and discuss how they would have undertaken this process. Compare your views with their own and explore carefully any differences between these. Think about what you have learned as a result of this process, about sampling children's achievements and analysing these systematically. What procedures or systems might you like to put in place to ensure this becomes a feature of your practice? Are there any changes, adaptations or recommendations you might suggest or make to the systems used already in the setting you are working in? Justify why you think these changes might be a helpful way forward.

Reporting to parents and carers

The concept of parents as partners in the education of their children is discussed in detail within the theme of 'Adults and children working together'. However, for the purposes of this discussion we need to focus on specific strategies that can be used to actively involve parents in the assessment and record keeping processes used within a Foundation Stage setting. Examples of children's play and learning at home can be used to add to school records of children's learning and development. This should enrich the view of the child as a 'whole being' whilst also recognising the important contribution that parents and carers can make to this process. Parents can be asked to make specific observations and assessments in the home setting, which can then contribute to records of achievement. Many Foundation Stage settings send games, puzzles and books home with children and parents or carers can be asked to comment on how the children used these. Parents can provide information about important events and achievements in the child's life at home, such as a new pet, or getting a gym award and so on. This is a dynamic partnership in which both parties (practitioners as well as parents and carers), have much to learn from one another. If this is a successful partnership then all those involved will feel valued and included but the children will also know that there is an important connection between their home life (which includes their community) and their school life. For further reading in this area refer to Fisher (2002, pages 22 to 28).

Preparation and task
Collect together detailed information on two children in your setting or class and compile an Annual Report to their parents using the report pro forma provided in the setting or school. This is a simulation and the report should **not** be presented to the actual parents, unless you are the practitioner in charge of the setting. Instead, show it to the lead practitioner or another colleague and discuss the detail of the content with them.

Evaluation and follow up
Evaluate what you have learned through this process and ask the practitioner if you might see some reports that other teachers have completed on children. These might need to be 'anonymised' to protect the confidentiality of the children, practitioner/teacher and parents.

Your achievements

Now you have read this section and completed the activities you should be able to:

➲ consider and evaluate the nature of the record keeping systems that need to be in place to support formative and summative assessment;
➲ reflect on the nature of the information that needs to be gathered and communicated between different personnel involved in supporting children in Foundation Stage settings, including their homes;
➲ consider strategies to involve parents as partners in all assessment and record keeping processes;
➲ consider how to involve children in the process of assessment and reflecting on their own learning;
➲ understand the statutory requirements for assessment, monitoring and reporting in the Foundation Stage;
➲ carry out a range of formative and summative assessment procedures;
➲ use the Foundation Profile to assess and record.

If you feel that you have completed the tasks successfully, return to the relevant needs analysis and mark it off with the date and evidence. If appropriate, ask your tutor about being able to use this as evidence of your understanding or professional capability. This information could be used as part of the course you are studying. This may be evidence towards the Professional Standards for QTS or it might be part of a profile or an assignment you might be completing as part of your studies. Please refer to the tables at the back of the book which detail coverage against the principles listed within the *Curriculum Guidance for the Foundation Stage* as well as the Professional Standards for QTS.

Chapter 5   Taking greater responsibility for, or within, the setting

Conclusion

Now that you have reached the end of this chapter you have had an opportunity to develop your professional knowledge, understanding and skills across all the themes so as to enable you to take responsibility within the setting. It is essential that you check you have evidence to support all the statements in the appropriate needs analysis table for this level. It is also important that you talk to your lead practitioner or school-based mentor at this stage. He or she will be able to help you check that you have appropriate evidence to audit your progress. If you are a trainee teacher you should also cross-reference this to the Professional Standards for QTS (see Appendix, **page 129**) and start to complete the profiling required by your training provider. You are now ready to develop your own practice further and take greater responsibility for or within the setting.

Chapter 6   Moving your learning forward

Your journey through this book will have been as a result of an interest in the care and education of young children. In the introduction, aspects of Foundation Stage provision were suggested as principles that should underpin your practice. It would be helpful now to revisit these and consider your response to them. This process of critical reflection is the basis of successful practice. As a newly qualified teacher (NQT), or as a teacher who has changed phases to work with children in the Foundation Stage, you now have the responsibility to further your theoretical and practical understanding in order to become the best possible practitioner.

If you are a trainee teacher, you will need to reflect on your achievements to date at the end of your training course. This will also require you to enter into a dialogue with your teachers and training provider tutors. The result of this process will be the completion of your Career Entry and Development Profile (CEDP) in consultation with your training provider. The CEDP will be used throughout your induction year to review your progress and drive the agenda for your continuing professional development. The evidence you collect throughout this induction year can then be used to begin your Professional Development Record. This should record your progress, performance and professional development needs, which will be reviewed on an annual basis through the performance management process. This process is one aspect of a DfES initiative to encourage and support teachers in continuing to update and share their knowledge, skills and practice in order to enhance children's learning. The DfES has provided a framework, which maps the different standards that apply at different stages of a teacher's career. It also includes ten dimensions of teaching and leadership that exist within a school, and you are encouraged to chart your progress against these as you move through your career. It is important for you to recognise your areas of expertise and achievements as well as identifying your development needs.

Whether you are a trainee or an experienced teacher, critical reflection is key to your success in working with young children. Children benefit from adults who understand their development and who are able to complement the curriculum requirements with challenging provision and a vision for children's individual goals. While reading the introduction you will have realised that the child is at the centre of the education process. Importance is then placed on the social setting, fostering self-esteem and security, ensuring that communication between adults and children is reciprocal and working with a curriculum that is developmentally appropriate.

As an early years practitioner, in whatever setting, you will be accountable to a number of stake holders including children, parents, the school, the governors, the local authority and the government. Reading the book and making progress through the tasks should have given you a framework upon which to start to develop increasingly secure and high quality early years practice. The lucid and succinct writing of Julie Fisher has been referred to at various points in the book. In a second book (Fisher, 2002b) she uses architectural analogies that liken the framework for the early years curriculum to the foundations of a building. In her conclusion she says that architects would never erect a building *without putting in the highest quality foundations, because the consequences would be too dire'* (Fisher 2002b, pages 127 to 128). Time, money and expertise are required for a professional job. *Money* may be out of your control but you will be able to take *time* to increase *expertise* and to continue to develop the observational, analytical and reflective skills that you needed to tackle the tasks for each theme in the book.

The most inspired early years practitioners are those who read, relate what they have read to their practice, and who have open and enquiring minds. In Chapter 5 you were urged to become a playful practitioner. This also implies continuing to be a learner as you respond to the colleagues, parents and, above all, the children you work with.

If you believe that the *'the early years are critical in children's development'* and that, *'the foundation stage of education will make a positive contribution to children's early development'* (QCA 2000, foreword) then the foundations of learning should be professionally constructed with every bit as much care taken in crafting and fashioning educational experience as is taken in constructing a building.

Your journey is just beginning! Take every opportunity to attend courses and conferences, keep in touch with the media, talk to colleagues and other practitioners, become active in early years organisations and continue your reading and research. Be prepared to stand up and be counted. Our young children are worth it!

Bibliography

Young children as learners and enquirers

Asprey, E, Hamilton, C and Haywood, S (2002) *Professional Issues in Primary Practice.* Exeter: Learning Matters.

Bruce, T (1997) *Early Childhood Education.* London: Hodder and Stoughton.

Bruce, T and Meggitt, C (1999) *Child Care and Education.* London: Hodder and Stoughton.

Department for Education and Science (1990) *Starting with Quality. The Report of the Committee of Inquiry into the Quality of the Educational Experiences Offered to 3- and 4-year-olds.* London: Routledge.

Donaldson, M (1978) *Children's Minds.* London: Fontana Press.

Dowling, M (1992) *Education 3-5.* London: Paul Chapman Publishing.

Edgington, M (1998) *The Nursery Teacher in Action.* London: Paul Chapman Publishing.

Fisher, J (2002) *Starting from the Child* (2nd edition). Buckingham: Open University Press.

Gardner, H (1983) *Frames of Mind: The Theory of Multiple Intelligences.* London: Fontana.

Goleman, D (1996) *Emotional Intelligence.* London: Bloomsbury Publishing Plc.

Greenfield, S (2001) *The Private Life of the Brain.* London: Penguin.

Katz, L (1998) in Smidt, S (1998) *Early Years. A Reader.* London: Routledge.

Laevers, F, Vandenbussche, E, Kog, M and Depondt, L (1994) *A Process-oriented Child Monitoring System for Young Children.* Belgium: Centre for Experiential Education.

Moyles, J, Adams, S and Musgrove, A (2002) *SPEEL Study of Pedagogical Effectiveness in Early Learning.* Nottingham: DfES.

QCA (2000) *The Curriculum Guidance for the Foundation Stage.* London: DfEE.

Sheridan, M (1997) *From Birth to Five Years.* London: Routledge.

Siraj-Blatchford, I, Sylva, K, Muttock, S, Gilden, R and Bell, D (2002) *Researching Effective Pedagogy in the Early Years.* Nottingham: DfES.

Smith, A (1996) *Accelerated Learning in the Classroom.* Stafford: Network Educational Press.

Tizard, B and Hughes, M (2002) *Young Children Learning* (2nd edition). Oxford: Blackwell Publishing.

Whitebread, D (2003) *Teaching and Learning in the Early Years* (2nd edition). London: Routledge Falmer.

Making connections in children's learning

Abbott, L and Nutbrown, C (2001) *Experiencing Reggio Emilia.* Buckingham: Open University Press.

Athey, C (1990) *Extending Thought in Young Children: A Parent–Teacher Partnership.* London: Paul Chapman Publishing.

Basic Skills Agency (2002) *Young Children's Skills on Entry to Education Survey 2002.* Cardiff: Beaufort Research Ltd.

Bruce, T (1991) *Time To Play in Early Childhood.* London: Hodder and Stoughton.

Bruce, T (1997) *Early Childhood Education.* London: Hodder and Stoughton.

Bruce, T (2001) *Learning Through Play.* London: Hodder and Stoughton.

Ceppi, G and Zini, M (eds) (1998) *Children, Spaces, Relations: Metaprojects for an Environment for Young Children.* Reggio Emilia, Italy: Reggio Children.

Craft, A (2000) *Creativity Across the Primary Curriculum.* London: Routledge.

David, T (ed) (1999) *Young Children Learning.* London: Paul Chapman Publishing.

Duffy, B (1998) *Supporting Creativity and Imagination in the Early Years.* Buckingham: Open University Press.

Duffy, B (2003) *Creativity Matters.* Presentation given at Birth to Three Matters Conference. 1 March, Manchester Metropolitan University, Didsbury Campus.

Edgington, M (1998) *The Nursery Teacher in Action.* London: Paul Chapman Publishing.

Edwards, C, Gandini, L and Forman, G (eds) (1998) *The Hundred Languages of Children.* Greenwich CT: Ablex Publishing Corporation.

Fisher, J (2002a) *Starting from the Child* (2nd edition). Buckingham: Open University Press.

Fisher, J (2002b) *The Foundations of Learning.* Buckingham: Open University Press.

Gale, M, Holloway, K and Roulstone, S (1995) *The Bristol Surveillance of Children's Communication (BRISC).* Bristol: United Bristol Healthcare NHS Trust.

Manning, K and Sharp, A (1977) *Structuring Play in the Early Years at School.* Sussex: Ward Lock Educational Co. Ltd.

Moyles, J (1989) *Just Playing.* Buckingham: Open University Press.

Moyles, J (ed) (1994) *The Excellence of Play*. Buckingham: Open University Press.

Moyles, J and Adams, S (2001) *STEPs Statements of Entitlement to Play. A Framework for Playful Teaching with 3-7-year-olds*. Buckingham: Open University Press.

QCA (2000) *Curriculum Guidance for the Foundation Stage*. London: DfEE.

POST (Parliamentary Office of Science and Technology) (2000) *Report on Early Years Learning*. London: POST. 140, Millbank.

Siraj-Blatchford, I (1998) *A Curriculum Development Handbook for Early Childhood Educators*. Staffordshire: Trentham Books.

Smidt, S (1998) *Early Years: A Reader*. London: Routledge.

The Early Childhood Education Forum (1998) *Quality in Diversity in Early Learning*. London: The National Children's Bureau.

Tizard, B and Hughes, M (2002) *Young Children Learning* (2nd edition). Oxford: Blackwell Publishing.

Wells, G (1996) *The Meaning Makers*. London: Hodder and Stoughton.

Adults and children working together

Athey, C (1990) *Extending Thought in Young Children: A Parent–Teacher Partnership*. London: Paul Chapman Publishing.

Drummond, M (1993) *Assessing Children's Learning*. London: David Fulton Publishers.

Lewis, M (2002) 'The Foundation Stage in England: A Dialogue Between Child and Educators, Parents and Teachers', in *Early Education* No 38, Autumn 2002, page 6.

Malaguzzi, L (1995) 'History Ideas and Basic Philosophy: An Interview with Lella Gandini' in Edwards, C, Gandini, L, and Forman, G (eds) *The Hundred Languages of Children: The Reggio Emilia Approach to Early Childhood Education*. Greenwich CT: Ablex Publishing.

Nutbrown, C (1999) *Threads of Thinking*. London: Paul Chapman Publishing

QCA, (2000) *Curriculum Guidance for the Foundation Stage*. London: DfEE.

Scottish Consultative Council on the Curriculum (1999) *A Curriculum Framework for Children Three to Five*. Edinburgh: The Scottish Office.

Smidt, S (1998) *Early Years: A Reader*. London: Routledge.

Whalley, M (2001) *Involving Parents in their Children's Learning*. London: Paul Chapman Publishing.

Willey, C (2001) 'Working with Parents in Early Years Settings', in Drury R, Miller, L, and Campbell, R *Looking at Early Years Education and Care*. London: David Fulton Publishers.

Organising the environment for learning

Asprey, E, Hamilton, C, and Haywood, S (2002) *Professional Issues in Primary Practice*. Exeter: Learning Matters.

Bilton, H (2002) *Outdoor Play in the Early Years. Management and Innovation* (2nd edition). London: David Fulton Publishers.

Bruce, T (1991) *Early Childhood Education*. London: Hodder and Stoughton.

Cadwell, L B (1997) *Bringing Reggio Emilia Home*. New York: Teachers College Press.

Curtis, A (1998) *A Curriculum for the Pre-school Child*. London: Routledge.

DfEE (1998) *The National Literacy Strategy*. London: HMSO.

DfEE/QCA (1999) *The National Numeracy Strategy*. London: HMSO.

QCA (2000) *Curriculum Guidance for the Foundation Stage*. London: DfEE

DfES (2002) *The National Numeracy Strategy Mathematical Activities for the Foundation Stage Introductory Pack*. London: DfES.

DfES (2003) *The National Literacy Strategy. Early Foundation Stage/Later Foundation Stage Medium-term Plans*. London: HMSO.

Edgington, M (1998) *The Nursery Teacher in Action* (2nd edition). London: Paul Chapman Publishing.

Edwards, C, Gandini, L and Forman, G (1998) *The Hundred Languages of Children. The Reggio Emilia Approach – Advanced Reflections* (2nd edition). London: Ablex Publishing Corporation

Fisher, J (2002a) *Starting from the Child* (2nd edition). Buckingham: Open University Press.

Fisher, J (ed) (2002b) *The Foundations of Learning*. Buckingham: Open University Press.

Hohman, M and Weikart, D (1995) *Educating Young Children*. Michigan: High Scope Press.

Moyles, J (ed) (1995) *Beginning Teaching: Beginning Learning in Primary Education*. Buckingham: Open University Press.

Pollard, A (1997) *Reflective Teaching in the Primary School – A Handbook for the Classroom* (3rd edition). London: Cassell.

Williams, J (2003) *Promoting Independent Learning in the Primary Classroom*. Buckingham: Open University Press.

Planning for learning

Bertram, T, Pascal, C, Paige-Smith, A, and Soler, J in Deveraux, J and Miller, L (2003*) Working with Children in the Early Years*. London: David Fulton Publishers.

Bilton, H (2002) *Outdoor Play in the Early Years. Management and Innovation* (2nd edition). London: David Fulton Publishers.

Brailsford, M, Hetherington, D, and Abram, E, 'Desirable Planning for Language and Literacy' in Marsh, J, and Hallet, E (1999) *Desirable Literacies: Approaches to Language and Literacy in the Early Years*. London: Paul Chapman Publishing.

Deveraux, J, and Miller, L, (2003) *Working with Children in the Early Years*. London: David Fulton Publishers.

DfEE (2001) *The National Literacy Strategy: Developing Early Writing*.

DfES (2003) *An Example of National Literacy Strategy Medium-term Planning*.

Fisher, J (2002) *Starting from the Child* (2nd edition). Buckingham: Open University Press.

Lasenby, M (1990) *The Early Years. A Curriculum for Young Children. Outdoor Play*. London: Harcourt Brace Jovanovich.

Macintyre, C (2001) *Enhancing Learning Through Play, A Developmental Perspective for Early Years Settings*. London: David Fulton.

Marsh, J, and Hallet, E (1999) *Desirable Literacies: Approaches to Language and Literacy in the Early Years*. London, Paul Chapman Publishing.

Miller L, Deveraux, J, Paige-Smith, A and Soler, J, 'Approaches to Curricula in the Early Years' in Deveraux, J and Miller, L (2003) *Working with Children in the Early Years*. London: David Fulton Publishers.

Montessori, M (1965) *Spontaneous Activity in Education*. Schocken Books: New York.

Moyles, J and Robinson, G (eds) (2002) *Beginning Teaching, Beginning Learning in Primary Education* (2nd edition). Buckingham: Open University Press.

Pascal, C and Bertram, T (1997) *Effective Early Learning, Case Studies in Improvement*. London: Hodder and Stoughton.

Pugh, G, 'The Consequences of Inadequate Investment in the Early Years' in Fisher, J (ed) (2002) *The Foundations of Learning*. Buckingham: Open University Press.

QCA (1997) *Looking at Children's Learning*. London: HMSO.

QCA (2000) *Curriculum Guidance for the Foundation Stage*. London: DfEE.

QCA (2001) *Planning for learning in the Foundation Stage*. London: DfEE.

Smidt, S (2002) *The Early Years, A Reader*. London: Routledge.

Webber, B in David, T (1999) *Young Children Learning*. London: Paul Chapman Publishing.

Whalley, M (2001) *Involving Parents in the Children's Learning*. London: Paul Chapman Publishing.

Whitbread, D (2003) *Teaching and Learning in the Early Years,* (2nd edition). London: Routledge Falmer.

Observing and assessing young children

Assessment Reform Group (1999) *Assessment for Learning: Beyond the Black Box*. University of Cambridge.

Athey, C (1990) *Extending Thought in Young Children: A Parent–Teacher Partnership*. London: Paul Chapman.

Black, P and Wiliam, D (1998) *Inside the Black Box*. London: King's College.

Bruce, T (1987) *Early Childhood Education*. Sevenoaks: Hodder and Stoughton.

Bruce, T (1991) *Time to Play in Early Childhood Education*. Sevenoaks: Hodder and Stoughton.

Department of Education and Science (1990) *Starting with Quality: Report of the Committee of Inquiry into the Educational Experiences Offered to Three and Four Year Olds* (The Rumbold Report). London: HMSO.

Drummond, M J (1994) *Assessing Children's Learning*. London: David Fulton.

Drummond, M J and Nutbrown, C (1996) 'Observing and Assessing Young Children' in Pugh, G (ed) *Contemporary Issues in the Early Years – Working Collaboratively for Children* (2nd edition). London: Paul Chapman Publishing, in association with the National Children's Bureau.

Ebbutt, S (1996) 'Assessing Numeracy' in Merttens, R (ed) (1996) *Teaching Numeracy: Maths in the Primary Classroom*. Leamington Spa: Scholastics Ltd.

Edgington, M (1998) *Keeping Records: Planning and Assessment in The Nursery Teacher in Action* (2nd edition). London: Paul Chapman Publishing.

Egersdorff, S (2002) 'Monitoring, Assessment, Recording, Reporting and Accountability: The Challenges for the Foundation Stage Teacher' in Keating, I (ed) (2002) *Teaching Foundation Stage*. Exeter: Learning Matters.

Fisher, J (2002) *Starting from the Child* (2nd edition). Buckingham: OUP.

Gardner, H (1993) *The Unschooled Mind: How Children Think and How Schools Should Teach*. London: Fontana.

Gipps, C (1994) *Beyond Testing*. London: Falmer Press.

Gipps, C and Stobart, G (1993) *Assessment: A Teachers' Guide to Issues*. London: Hodder and Stoughton.

Headington, R (2000) *Monitoring, Assessment, Recording, Reporting and Accountability. Meeting the Standards*. London: Fulton.

Hohman, M and Weikart, D (1995) *Educating Young Children*. Michigan: High Scope Press.

Holt, J (1982) *How Children Fail* (2nd edition). Harmondsworth: Penguin.

Hurst, V and Lally, M (1992) 'Assessment and the Nursery Curriculum' in Blenkin, G and Kelly, A (eds) *Assessment in Early Childhood Education*. London: Paul Chapman.

Hurst, V (1996) 'Parents and Professionals: Partnership in Early Childhood Education' in Blenkin, G and Kelly, A (eds) *Early Childhood Education: A Developmental Approach* (2nd edition). London: Paul Chapman.

Keating, I (ed) (2002) *Teaching Foundation Stage*. Exeter: Learning Matters.

Lindsay, G (1998) 'Baseline assessment: a positive or malign initiative?' in Norwich, B and Lindsay, G (eds) *Baseline Assessment: Practice, Benefits and Pitfalls?* Tamworth: NASEN.

Pascal, C and Bertram, A (1996) *Effective Early Learning Research Project.* Worcester: Amber Publishing.

Pugh, G (ed) (1996) *Contemporary Issues in the Early Years – Working Collaboratively for Children* (2nd edition). London: Paul Chapman Publishing, in association with the National Children's Bureau.

Mitchell, C and Koshy, V (1993) *Effective Teacher Assessment: Looking at Children's Learning in the Primary Classroom.* London: Hodder and Stoughton.

Nutbrown, C (1994) *Threads of Thinking – Young Children Learning and the Role of Early Education.* London: Paul Chapman.

QCA (2000) *Curriculum Guidance for the Foundation Stage.* London: DfEE.

QCA (2003) *Foundation Stage Profile, Handbook.* London: DfES.

Smidt, S (1998) *A Guide to Early Years Practice.* London: Routledge.

Sparks, Linfield R and Warwick, P (2003) '"Is it Like a School Bus?" Assessment in the Early Years' in Whitebread, D (ed) *Teaching and Learning in the Early Years* (2nd edition). London: Routledge Falmer.

Standards

DfES/TTA (2002) *Qualifying to Teach: Professional Standards for Qualified Teacher Status and Requirements for Initial Teacher Training.* London: HMSO.

Appendix

Table 1 summarises this book's coverage of the principles identified in the *Curriculum Guidance for the Foundation Stage* (QCA, 2000).

Table 2 details the links between the themes covered in this book and the Professional Standards for Qualified Teacher Status. The Standards for the Award of Qualified Teacher Status are outcome statements that set out what a trainee teacher must know, understand and be able to do to be awarded QTS. You can access the complete set of Standards at www.tta.gov.uk/training/qtsstandards/.

Table 1

Principles included in the *Curriculum Guidance for the Foundation Stage*	Coverage
Effective education requires both a relevant curriculum and practitioners who understand and are able to implement the curriculum requirements.	Organising the environment for learning, Chapters 3,4,5 Planning for learning, Chapters 2 and 3
Effective education requires practitioners who understand that children develop rapidly during the early years – physically, intellectually, emotionally and socially.	Young children as learners and enquirers, Chapter 2
Practitioners should ensure that all children feel included, secure and valued.	Organising the environment for learning, Chapter 2 Adults and children working together, Chapters 2 and 3
Early years experience should build on what children already know and can do.	Young children as learners and enquirers, Chapter 4 Organising the environment for learning, Chapter 5 Planning for learning, Chapter 4
No child should be excluded or disadvantaged because of ethnicity, culture or religion, home language, family background, special educational needs, disability, gender or ability.	Organising the environment for learning, Chapter 2 Adults and children working together, Chapters 3, 4 and 5 Planning for learning, Chapters 4 and 5
Parents and practitioners should work together in an atmosphere of mutual respect within which children can have security and confidence.	Organising the environment for learning, Chapter 5 Adults and children working together, Chapters 2 and 4
To be effective, an early years curriculum should be carefully structured.	Planning for learning, Chapters 2,3,4 and 5
There should be opportunities for children to engage in activities planned by adults and also those that they plan or initiate themselves.	Organising the environment for learning, Chapter 4 Planning for learning, Chapter 4
Practitioners must be able to observe and respond appropriately to children, informed by a knowledge of how children develop and learn and a clear understanding of possible next steps in their development and learning.	Observing and assessing young children, Chapters 2, 3, 4 & 5
Well-planned, purposeful activity and appropriate intervention by practitioners will engage children in the learning process and help them make progress in their learning.	Planning for learning, Chapters 2,3,4 and 5 Observing and assessing young children, Chapters 2, 3, 4 & 5
For children to have rich and stimulating experiences, the learning environment should be well planned and well organised.	Organising the environment for learning, Chapters 3, 4 and 5,
Effective learning and development for young children requires high-quality care and education by practitioners.	All themes

Table 2

Young children as learners and enquirers	
Standards covered within this theme 1.2, 1.3, 1.6, 1.7 2.1a, 2.4, 3.3.1	
Specific standards covered in each chapter	
Making sense of the setting	2.1a, 2.4, 3.3.1
Making a contribution to the setting	1.3, 1.7 2.1a, 2.4 3.3.1
Taking greater responsibility for or within the setting	1.6 2.1a

Making connections in children's learning	
Standards covered within this theme 1.6, 1.7 2.1a 3.3.2a	
Specific standards covered in each chapter	
Making sense of the setting	2.1a 3.3.2a
Making a contribution to the setting	1.7 2.1a 3.3.2a
Taking greater responsibility for or within the setting	1.6 2.1a 3.3.2a

Adults and children working together	
Standards covered within this theme 1.1, 1.2, 1.3, 1.4, 1.6, 1.8 2.2, 2.4, 3.1.3, 3.1.4, 3.1.5, 3.2.5 3.3.1, 3.3.5, 3.3.6, 3.3.12 3.3.13, 3.3.14	
Specific standards covered in each chapter	
Making sense of the setting	1.1 1.2, 1.3 2.4 3.2.5 3.3.1, 3.3.14
Making a contribution to the setting	1.4, 1.6 2.4 3.1.3, 3.1.4, 3.3.5, 3.3.6, 3.3.12, 3.3.13
Taking greater responsibility for or within the setting	1.6 3.1.4 3.1.5

Organising the environment for learning

Standards covered within this theme
1.3, 1.7
2.7
3.1.3 3.3.1 3.3.3 3.3.8 3.3.9 3.3.13

Specific standards covered in each chapter

Making sense of the setting	3.3.1 3.3.9
Making a contribution to the setting	3.1.3 3.3.1 3.3.3 3.3.8
Taking greater responsibility for or within the setting	1.3 1.7 2.7 3.3.8 3.3.13

Planning for learning

Standards covered within this theme
1.1, 1.6, 1.7,
2.1a
3.1, 3.1.2, 3.1.3, 3.1.4, 3.1.5, 3.3.3

Specific standards covered in each chapter

Making sense of the setting	
Making a contribution to the setting	1.1, 1.7, 2.1a 3.1, 3.1.2, 3.1.3, 3.1.4, 3.1.5, 3.3.3
Taking greater responsibility for or within the setting	1.1, 1.6, 1.7, 2.1a 3.1, 3.1.2, 3.1.3, 3.1.4, 3.1.5, 3.3.3

Observing and assessing young children

Standards covered within this theme
1.1, 1.2, 1.4, 1.6,
2.1a,
3.1.1, 3.1.2, 3.2.1, 3.2.2, 3.2.3, 3.2.4, 3.2.6, 3.2.7, 3.3.4, 3.3.6,

Specific standards covered in each chapter

Making sense of the setting	3.2.1,
Making a contribution to the setting	3.2.1, 3.2.2, 3.2.4
Taking greater responsibility for or within the setting	3.2.3. 3.2.4, 3.2.6, 3.2.7

Index